D1489777

British Honduras to Belize: Transformation of a Nation

Godfrey Mwakikagile

1

British Honduras to Belize: Transformation of a Nation
Godfrey Mwakikagile

First Edition

ISBN 978-9987-16-047-1

New Africa Press
Dar es Salaam, Tanzania

Contents

Introduction

THIS is not a definitive work on Belize. But it's comprehensive enough for the general reader to know some basic facts about the country.

Belize is one of the most interesting places in Latin America. And it has a unique history in the region.

Even in contemporary times, its strong ties to the Caribbean, although it's a Central American nation, are some of its most distinctive characteristics among the countries of Central and South America, besides Guyana which was also once ruled by Britain.

When I came up with the idea of writing this book, I had three groups of people in mind: tourists and other travellers who are interested in going to Belize; members of the general public who don't even intend to go to Belize; and students who know very little or nothing about this Central American country.

There are many guide books which have been written about Belize. This one does not pretend to be one of those books, let alone a comprehensive one, about the country. Such books cover a lot more than what's contained in this work.

But I hope that my work will also help some tourists and other travellers to learn some basic facts about the land, the history, the people, and the culture of this country. In that sense, it serves as a general introduction to Belize.

Students who are learning about Belize for the first time may find this book to be equally useful in that sense. It may also inspire them to learn even more about the country by reading more comprehensive works, in terms of scope and depth, on this Central American nation.

Members of the general public who simply want to know a few basic facts about Belize will probably find this work to be comprehensive enough in that respect as well. The facts provided here may also encourage them to learn more about the country perhaps as much as they do about other countries.

People from all walks of life go to Belize for different reasons. But many of them are united by a common objective: to learn about the country before they go there. I hope that this work will help at least some of them achieve that goal.

Subjects covered include the country's cultural and ethnic diversity, as well as its political landscape, constituting a vibrant heterogeneous society that is also unique in the Central American region as the only country that was once ruled by Britain.

It has its shortcomings like all works by mere mortals. But it's comprehensive enough, in scope even if not in depth, as a compilation of basic facts about this fascinating Central American nation.

The work was originally published as *Belize and its Identity: A Multicultural Perspective* and then as *Belize and Its People: Life in A Multicultural Society*. But it has been revised and does not contain some of the material found in the other works.

Part One:

Belize: General Background

BELIZE is a small country in Central America. It's bordered by Mexico on the north and northwest, by Guatemala on the south and southwest, and by the Caribbean Sea on the east.

It's located along the coast in the eastern part of Central America and is separated by sea from Honduras, its neighbour on the southwest.

It has an area of about 8,870 square miles and had a population of more than 322,100 in 2008.

Belize's population density is the lowest in Central America. It's also one of the lowest in the world. But its population growth rate is the highest in the region and one of the highest in the Western hemisphere.

Its population increased sharply in the 1980s when a very large number of illegal immigrants entered Belize from Guatemala, El Salvador Honduras, and Nicaragua when those countries were embroiled in conflicts including civil wars.

This wave of immigrants changed the demographic

balance in the country. Belize also earned the distinction of having one of the highest percentages of illegal immigrants in the world.

The immigrants constituted about 15 to 20 per cent of the country's population. One out of every six persons in Belize was an illegal immigrant.

In terms of raw numbers, the country ended up having an additional 60,000 people by the 1990s, most of them illegal immigrants from Guatemala, Honduras, El Salvador, and also from Mexico.

The mainland of Belize is about 180 miles long and up to 68 miles wide. Belize also has more than 450 islands. The size of the islands varies greatly, ranging from a few hundred feet to 25 miles long and 4 miles wide.

Most of the islands are located inside the 200-mile Belize Barrier Reef. The reef serves as a buffer against devastating winds and waves of the Caribbean Sea which is part of the Atlantic Ocean.

The coastline is flat and swampy. And the country's interior has low mountains.

Belize has a subtropical climate of dry and wet seasons. It's hot and humid.

The rainy season starts in June and ends in November. But in some parts of the country, rains starts in May. The month of May also is the hottest in Belize; the coldest is January.

English is the official language. But Spanish also is widely spoken.

Other languages include Kriol which is a dialect of English and mainly a product of the descendants of African slaves; Garifuna which is based on the Arawak language of the Amerindian indigenous people of the Caribbean islands and sprinkled with African words and idioms; Mayan languages; German spoken mostly by Mennonites; Chinese; Hindi spoken by immigrants from India; Arabic; and Turkish.

Belize was once a British colony known as British

Honduras. And it's the only country in Central America which uses English as the official language.

It's also the only country in Central America with a British colonial heritage. The rest are Spanish.

Although geographically it's a Central American country, it has strong ties to the island nations of the Caribbean.

The ties have been forged and reinforced by a common racial heritage of Belize's black population and of the island nations which are also predominantly black.

They have a common African origin. The countries also have a common history of slavery and as former British colonies.

Although it's a small country, Belize is known for its ethnic, racial and cultural diversity. It's the most heterogeneous society in Central America.

It also has a long history, not necessarily as a country that came to be known as Belize but as a geographical and cultural region.

The area that came to be known as Belize was an integral part of the Maya empire. The Maya civilisation spread into the area which is known as Belize today between 1500 B.C. and 300 A.D. It flourished until about 1200 A.D., although there is a dispute over that. Some historians say it thrived until 800 A.D.

The name Belize itself is believed to be of Mayan origin. The Mayan word, *belix*, means "muddy water." It's a term used to describe what is now known as Belize River.

When the Mayan civilisation came into existence about 3,000 years ago, it covered the lowlands and highland areas of what is now southeastern Mexico, Guatemala, western Honduras, and Belize. And the continued existence of cultural vestiges and physical monuments of this magnificent civilisation even after 500 years of domination by its European conquerors is an enduring testimony to its resilience and achievements.

Before 2500 B.C., various groups of the Maya settled in small villages in this large region. Some were hunters and others were farmers. And there were also those who survived by moving from place to place, foraging, for survival.

The groups eventually got together and formed communities which engaged in farming.

That was the beginning of organised farming in the region, and the people later started growing on regular basis crops such as maize, beans and chili peppers.

The Maya were among the first people in the world to grow maize which was later taken to other parts round the globe.

Through the centuries, a variety of languages and distinct subcultures developed in the region which collectively constituted the Mayan civilisation. This evolution was one of the distinct features of this great civilisation.

The native people did not belong to one ethnic group, and different identities among them persisted through the centuries although they all belonged to the same civilisation.

Basic institutions of the Mayan civilisation, including institutional structures of governance and religion as well as economic development, evolved between 2500 B.C. and 250 A.D. The civilisation reached its peak during the classic period which began around 250 A.D.

During the latter part of the Mayan empire before 1000 A.D., about 400,000 people lived in the region that's now known as Belize.

People established villages and other communal settlements in almost every part of the country where they could farm and grow crops. They also settled in the island and coastal swampy areas in the eastern part of what's now Belize.

But something happened in the 10th century.

The Mayan civilisation experienced a major decline

which amounted to a breakdown of the Mayan society. It was the beginning of the end of one of the most significant and most advanced civilisations in the history of mankind during that period.

Construction of public buildings as well as other infrastructure and institutions stopped. The administrative centres which helped to hold the society together lost power.

These administrative centres collectively constituted the central authority of the Mayan civilisation. The centre could no longer hold the empire together.

There was also a major decline in the Mayan population. The social and economic structures which had worked so well through the centuries lost their functional utility.

Some people continued to occupy and may even have reoccupied sites such as Altún Ha, Xunantunich, and Lamanai. Still, these sites were no longer what they used to be as centres of the Mayan civilisation.

The rise and fall of Mayan civilisation has never been fully explained and questions still remain:

How did the people of that era learn advanced astronomy and mathematics? Where did this knowledge come from?

Why were they so far ahead of other people in the region and elsewhere in different parts of the world?

What caused the dramatic decline of this magnificent civilisation? Was there a single cause or was it a combination of factors?

And did it really fall abruptly in only a few years? Or did it collapse after almost a century?

Experts differ on that.

Instead of attributing the decline of the Mayan civilisation to a single cause, many archaeologists now believe that its decline was a result of many complex factors. They also believe that the decline occurred at different times in different regions.

But there is no question that during its period, it was a highly advanced civilisation even by modern standards in some areas such as architecture, astronomy and mathematics. Several major archaeological sites which exist even today are a living monument to that wonderful civilisation.

The Mayan empire also had a much denser population for that era in human history, contrasted with many other societies around the world during the same period.

Besides the archaeological sites such as Caracol, Lamanai, Lubaantun, Altun Ha, and Xunantunich which still exist today, there are many others, although not well-known, but no less important.

But in spite of its splendid achievements, the foundation of this civilisation was, in one way, an open secret. And it could not have existed, let alone thrived, without it. The question is why the Mayan society was able to develop and achieve phenomenal growth while others in the region remained behind or stagnant.

More than anything else, the Mayan civilisation was based on agriculture, as was the case with other civilisations in other parts of the world during that period. The Maya – or Mayans – engaged in a variety of agricultural activities and developed several ways to improve farming.

Their farming methods were relatively advanced for that period compared with other societies in different parts of the world.

They developed a fairly complex irrigation system which was labour-intensive.

They also used ridged-field systems to retain fertile soil and water and enable plants to grow well without shortage of water and good soil which could easily have been washed away by rain and rivers without the ridges.

The Maya also used shifting cultivation and slash-and-burn techniques.

In shifting cultivation, land is used temporarily, or

periodically, so that the fields which were previously used to grow crops are left fallow.

Shifting cultivation sometimes involves both people and crops. Both shift.

The people move to a new settlement while the land is left to "rest" or regain its vitality. But a lot of times, it's only the land which is shifted, or cultivated temporarily, while the people remain in the same villages or settlements and then go to the land to farm and grow crops.

Slashing-and-burning techniques involve cutting and burning grass and forests to clear the land for farming and are sometimes used together with shifting cultivation.

All these farming methods helped to develop and sustain the Mayan civilisation for centuries.

The Mayan empire had many highly skilled people. The included specialists in different areas. Many were craftsmen and merchants. There were also warriors, and priest-astronomers who coordinated agricultural and other activities based on seasons. They performed rituals based on the Mayan calendar. These rituals were performed at designated centres where religious activities and other ceremonial activities took place.

The priest-astronomers were great experts in the field of astronomy even if, by modern standards, they had only rudimentary knowledge in some areas. But they were able to track the movements of the sun, the moon, the planets, and the stars. They also developed a highly advanced system of calendar and mathematics which enabled them to record time and events. The records were kept on carved stones and sometimes on wooden slabs using Mayan writing.

The large number of these slabs – also known as stelae – which still exist in Central America constitute one of the largest and most significant sources of information on that civilisation.

The Maya were also highly skilled in making pottery and carving jade. They also made elaborate costumes of feathers for religious ceremonies and daily use.

Their advanced architecture was noted for its temples and magnificent residential buildings made of stone. They were well-decorated with paintings and complex geometric patterns. The arrangement of the buildings themselves followed a geometric pattern.

It was all the product of an advanced civilisation whose achievements in fields such as astronomy and mathematics still baffle experts today.

The majestic ruins and other sites of magnificent splendour are now an important part of Belize's cultural heritage and history even though there was no country known as Belize back then, and even though the majority of the people in Belize today are not descended from that civlisation.

Many items have been recovered from that old civilisation. They include bowls, jars and other items which are among the oldest found in the region of Central America and of what is now Mexico.

The collapse of the Maya civilisation was probably the most critical event in the history of the Maya people since the founding of their civlisation.

Another major event of equal importance in terms of impact on the lives of the Maya was the arrival of Europeans in the 1500s A.D. Their lives changed forever.

When Europeans first arrived in what is now called Central America, there were some Mayans still living in the lowland areas of what is Belize today.

Research including archaeological evidence shows that there were different groups of the Maya in the 1700s in the area now known as Belize.

But the Maya territory covered more than that. Besides what is now Belize, it also included parts of Mexico and Guatemala.

The first European to arrive in the region was Christopher Columbus. That was in 1502 when he sailed along the coast of what's now Belize and other parts of

Central America. He explored the coastal area of Belize as did other explorers from Spain.

Spain had the upper hand during that period and sent expeditions to the area of what is now Guatemala and Honduras. It was the dawn of a new era in the history of the region, and the conquest of Yucatán began in 1527.

The Maya fought back, putting up stiff resistance against the European invaders who described their campaign as "pacification" of the indigenous people whom they considered to be inferior to them.

But resistance by the native population was not successful because of their inferior technology. Their crude weapons were no match for European guns.

Their resistance was also compromised by another weakness: vulnerability to disease.

The diseases, some of them unheard of, devastated the indigenous population and weakened its ability to resist conquest. The diseases were brought from Europe by the Spanish invaders and the Maya had no resistance to the new infections. The result was catastrophic.

Permanent European settlement was also facilitated by the propagation of a new faith in the region. Spanish missionaries established churches in Mayan settlements in the 1600s to covert the people to Christianity.

But for the Spanish rulers, and even for some of the missionaries, there was another motive behind such proselytisation. And that was subjugation and control of the indigenous population to make them docile by convincing them to wait for their pie in the sky while their conquerors enjoyed theirs right here and now.

There were some white missionaries who were true Christians, but not all of them were.

Other colonised people had the same experience and discerned the same ulterior motives, although there were some missionaries who had good intentions in other parts of the world as well. As Jomo Kenyatta, who was accused of leading Mau Mau in Kenya, once said: "The white man came and told us, 'Shut your eyes, let us pray.' When we opened our eyes, it was too late. Our land was gone."

The fate of the Maya centuries earlier was not much different from what befell Africans and other conquered people in different parts of the world.

While the Spanish conquistadors were consolidating their rule in the territories they had conquered in Central America, another enterprise was taking place during the same period. And that was piracy. It became a thriving business in the region and the area that is now Belize was one of the focal points of this activity.

Some Spanish settlers tried to establish settlements in the interior of what is now Belize but they were repelled by the Maya. The attacks forced them to abandon their settlement scheme in the area. But they succeeded in establishing settlements elsewhere in Central America and South America.

In the 1700s and 1800s, Spain tried to maintain a monopoly on trade and colonisation in its colonial territories in Central America. But northern European powers were equally interested in the region. They wanted to establish their own colonies in Central and South America and in the Caribbean. They also wanted to conduct trade.

The northern European powers – Britain, France and The Netherlands (Holland) – entered the region determined to thwart attempts by Spain to become the dominant power in the area. They used a combination of tactics including war to achieve this goal. They also engaged in piracy and smuggling.

The 1800s were a turning point in the history of colonial conquest of the region. It was during this period that the Dutch, English and French seriously challenged Spain in Central America. One of those areas was Belize as it came to be known later.

The first Europeans to establish a settlement in the area that is now Belize were British. That was in 1638, an important milestone in the history of Belize. They were mostly from England. But there were also settlers from Scotland.

During the first part of the 1600s, buccaneers from England got involved in the lumber business for the first time in the region. They began cutting logwood in the southern part of Mexico and on the Yucatán Peninsula, introducing a new enterprise that was to determine the history of the region for centuries.

There is a legend which says one of the buccaneers, Peter Wallace, is the one who gave his name to the largest river in Belize in 1638. The name of Belize River is said to have come from Peter Wallace's nickname. The Spanish settlers reportedly called him "Ballis," hence Belize River, and Belize the country as it is known today. Another source of the name is, of course, said to be Mayan as we learned earlier.

The buccaneers were known as Baymen. They first settled along the coast of Belize in order to have a vantage point from which they could attack Spanish ships in order to drive the Spaniards out of the region. The Spanish ships carried mainly logwood during that period.

But later, the buccaneers stopped attacking Spanish ships and started cutting their own wood in the 1650s and 1660s.

The sale of logwood formed the foundation of the British settlement in what is now Belize. And it helped to sustain the settlement for more than one hundred years.

Involvement in the logwood industry was also facilitated by an agreement signed by the European powers in 1667. Spain, Britain and other European powers competing in the region agreed to work together to end piracy in the area.

This encouraged the British settlers in Belize to stop piracy and start cutting logwood. It was a lucrative business for them and it changed the history of the region. It was the Baymen – former pirates and now logwood cutters – who paved the way for the establishment of what later became the colony of British Honduras, now known as Belize.

The first Baymen settled in an area that became Belize City in the 1650s. They settled mainly in the northern part of the city – before it became a city and when it was just an open area.

During the next 150 years, after the first settlements were established in 1638, more English settlements were established in the area. This was also a period piracy and attacks by Indians and by Spanish settlers in surrounding areas who wanted the British out of there.

The Baymen tried to neutralise the Spanish settlers in Mexico and Central America without much success.

But they did earn a living cutting and selling logwood which played a major role not only in the establishment but also in the survival of the British colony.

And although the powers involved – especially Britain and Spain – agreed to contain and end piracy, it did not mean an end to competition and rivalry between these powers in the region of Central America. Conflict continued, and sometimes even escalated, between Britain and Spain over the rights of the British to cut wood and settle in the region.

During the 1700s, Spanish forces attacked the British settlers repeatedly in the area that is now Belize But Spanish settlers never settled in the region, and the British always returned to expand their trade and settlement.

The Treaty of Paris signed in 1763 conceded to Britain the right to cut logwood but asserted Spanish sovereignty over the territory, although not in a clearly defined way as we will learn later.

When war broke out again in 1779, the British settlement was abandoned until the Treaty of Versailles signed in 1783 allowed the British again to cut logwood in the area. But by that time, the logwood trade had declined significantly and the Honduras mahogany became the main export.

However, the logwood trade can not be underestimated in the role it played in the founding of Belize as a country and as a nation. Its role was also unique in the history of the region because of its origin.

Logwood is native to southern Mexico and northern Central America. It has been of great economic value for many years. And what is Belize today as a country and as nation would probably not be what it is today had it not been for this tree. The country grew from logging camps established by the British – especially the English and to a smaller extent the Scottish – during the 1600s. Their activities intensified in the 1700s.

The wood produced a fixing agent for clothing dyes that was vital to the European woolen industry.

For many years, logwood continued to be used as the main source of dye. And it's still important today. The bark and the leaves are used for medical purposes in a number of areas.

During the early years of European settlement in the region, the dye from logwood was very important and was widely used not only in the production of textiles but also in the production of paper. And the history of Belize is inextricably linked with these products besides the tree itself.

The first British settlers also played a role in shaping the events which would later determine how the British settlement would be administered as a colony.

After the English and Scottish buccaneers and pirates settled in the northern part of what is now Belize City, they became very powerful in the administration of this urban settlement.

In the late 1700s, an oligarchy of relatively wealthy British settlers controlled the economy of the British settlement. They were also the dominant political force in this settlement. They owned about four-fifths of the land; owned about half of all the slaves; controlled imports, exports, and the wholesale and retail trades; and imposed taxes on their own terms.

Also, a group of magistrates whom they elected from among themselves had executive as well as judicial functions over the British settlement. And they resisted any challenge to their growing political power derived from the wealth they had.

They controlled the municipal government and later the national government itself since the town constituted the nucleus of the new colony.

And it was they who controlled the system of slavery in Belize. They used African slaves to cut logwood and do other work. Some of the slaves escaped but ended up under new masters, the Spanish settlers in neighbouring countries such as Guatemala.

The British settlers in Belize also had to find ways to maintain their control over their African slaves. The settlers were few and they were outnumbered by the slaves.

One way the settlers maintained effective control over their African slaves was by separating them from the growing population of free blacks who were given limited privileges. These blacks were known as Kriols, descendants of African slaves.

Although some Kriols were legally free, their economic freedom and voting rights were severely restricted. However, whatever privileges they enjoyed, and however limited, encouraged them to embrace British culture and pledge loyalty to Britain. They literally saw themselves as black Englishmen or Englishmen only with a black or nonwhite skin.

The slaves were finally freed by the British in 1838 but still lived as second-class citizens in Belize. And in 1840, the colony of British Honduras, what is Belize today, was formally declared.

The law abolishing slavery was intended to avoid drastic social changes in the British settlement.

It was enforced slowly or gradually by carrying out emancipation over a five-year transition period; by implementing a system of "apprenticeship" intended to extend masters' control over the former slaves; and by compensating former slave owners for their loss of property.

Slaves were considered property like furniture. They were not even considered to be full human beings. For example, in the United States, they were considered to be three-fifth of a human being, not much different from what they were in Belize.

After 1838, the people who controlled the British settlement in Belize continued to dominate the country for more than a century. And they denied freed slaves access to land and severely limited their freedom in all areas of life.

At the same time that the British settlers in Belize were thinking how to deal with the end of slavery, and whatever problems may arise from this fundamental change, a new ethnic group, the Garifuna, emerged on the scene in another part of the British empire but with profound implication for the future of Belize.

The terms "Garifuna" and "Garinagu" are sometimes used interchangeably although there is a technical difference between the two, with "Garinagu" being the plural form of "Garifuna." But "Garifuna" is now the preferred term even in plural form.

In the early 1800s, the Garifunas – or Garinagu – who were descendants of Carib peoples of the Lesser Antilles and of Africans who had escaped from slavery, arrived in the British settlement of Belize.

The Garifunas resisted British and French colonial rule and oppression in the Lesser Antilles until they were defeated by the British in 1796.

After suppressing an uprising by the Garifuna on the island of Saint Vincent, the British colonial rulers moved between 1,700 and 5,000 of them to Central America.

23

They were forced to settle on the Bay Islands – what is now Islas de la Bahía – off the northern coast of Honduras.

They later left the Bay Islands in search of a new home. Different groups eventually settled in the Caribbean coastal areas of Nicaragua, Honduras, Guatemala, and the southern part of what is now Belize.

By 1802, about 150 Garifunas had settled in the Stann Creek area in southern Belize, especially in Dangriga, where they became involved in fishing and farming. They are among the best fishermen in Belize today and have been for many years.

Years later, other Garifunas migrated to the British settlement in Belize, fleeing from civil war in Honduras in 1832. Many Garifuna men soon found jobs in the forestry industry cutting mahogany together with the slaves.

In 1841 – about a year after the colony of British Honduras was established – Dangriga was a flourishing village. It was the largest Garifuna settlement in Belize; and it is still one today. There was another thriving Garifuna settlement in Punta Gorda, also in southern Belize, with many successful farmers.

But the British settlers in Belize did not treat the Garifunas as equal residents or citizens. They treated them as squatters.

In 1857 the British told the Garifunas that they must obtain leases from the Crown or risk losing their property including land and houses.

It was blatant racism.

But African slaves and other groups – including the Garifuna who are also partly African – were not the only people who suffered at the hands of the European settlers. The indigenous people also suffered immensely.

Their land was taken away from them. They were enslaved and exploited. And their traditional way of life was profoundly affected by the intrusion of foreigners from Europe who also regarded them as inferior to whites;

a common experience of colonial subjects at the hands of their conquerors around the world.

In the area that is now Belize, the Maya suffered and died under Spanish occupation. They were massacred and fled into the dense forests of central and western Belize for security.

The British buccaneers and pirates also attacked the Maya along the coast of Belize. They raided and destroyed most of the Mayan settlements along the coast. They also stole food, enslaved the Maya, and kidnapped Mayan women and children.

Some Mayans were even sold as slaves to British plantation owners and settlers in Jamaica. Some were also sold to slave masters in the southern states of the United States, especially North Carolina, South Carolina, and Virginia.

The region was a land of suffering for nonwhites but also of prosperity for settlers from Europe.

Attempts were also made to improve relations between the rival European powers in the region when Spain granted the British settlers the right to occupy the area that is now Belize. Spain also allowed the British settlers to cut logwood in exchange for an end to piracy, while slavery continued.

From the early 1700s, African slaves were shipped from Jamaica to Belize to cut logwood and do other slave work for the British settlers.

The earliest written record about African slaves in the British settlement of Belize is an account by a Spanish missionary in 1724 in which he stated that the British had recently been importing slaves from Jamaica, Bermuda and other British colonies in the region.

A century later, the number of African slaves in what is now Belize reached 2,300.

Most of the slaves were born in Africa. And many of them knew which tribes they came from. They also continued to follow their African way of life in a number of areas including observing customs and traditions. Even the way they socialised, prayed, sang, danced and cooked had echoes from the past traced all the way back to where they came from.

But as time went on, they embraced British culture while at the same maintaining some aspects of their African way of life. Cultural fusion took place and the result was a new culture, Kriol, and a new people also known as Kriol, although the culture was predominantly British as it still is today among the Kriol (Creole) in Belize.

However, the influence of African slaves and those who were later set free can not be underestimated in the history of Belize.

In fact, as early as 1800, African slaves outnumbered British settlers in Belize by about four to one.

By then, the settlement's primary export had shifted from logwood to mahogany. And as Professor Nigel O. Bolland of Colgate University, New York, states in his book *Colonialism and Resistance in Belize: Essays in Historical Sociology*:

"The principal establishment was located at the Belize River mouth. This settlement grew into Belize City.

In the nineteenth century, Belize Town, which in 1881 consisted of 5,767 persons (about 21 per cent of the colony's population), remained a small town. It was, and still is, the centre of concentration of Belize's Creole population: over 60 per cent of the 45,584 inhabitants of Belize City today are Creole.

Whatever the date at which Africans first appeared in Belize, they certainly outnumbered the white settlers by the middle of the eighteenth century.

A description of the settlement in 1799, a few days before St. George's Cay was captured, stated there were about 500 British settlers and 3,000 slaves.

After the resettlement, 2,214 people, three-quarters of

them slaves, were evacuated to Belize from the Mosquito Shore. Some of these were settled in Convention Town, which was established on the south point of the Belize River mouth.

Censuses taken in 1790 indicate that there were about 2,200 slaves and about 400 'free people of colour' in a total population of less than 3,000.

Most of these people were engaged in cutting logwood and mahogany up the various rivers and creeks, principally the Belize, Sibun, New, and Northern rivers, but their principal settlement, to which the woodcutters returned at the end of of each logging session, remained Belize Town (Bolland 1977: 25 – 48).

The economy largely determined this pattern of settlement. Woodcutters were required to spend several months living in isolation in temporary makeshift camps in the forest." – (Nigel O. Bolland, *Colonialism and Resistance in Belize: Essays in Historical Sociology*, Benque Viejo del Carmen, Belize: Cubola Productions, 3rd Edition, 1 June 2004, pp.79 – 80).

Although African slaves were an integral part of the economy from the beginning starting with the logwood industry and were, in fact, indispensable, they were treated as if they were on the periphery of the economic mainstream because they had no power. And they were not allowed to own land.

They were victims of blatant discrimination. And as slaves, they could not be equal to their masters. But even freed blacks were treated the same. Land ownership was concentrated in the hands of only a few whites. As Bolland goes on to state:

"By the late eighteenth century, a small group of between twelve and twenty 'old Baymen,' as they styled themselves, owned over half of all slaves in the settlement and had allocated vast tracts of land to themselves. This 'monopoly on the part of the monied cutters' was unsuccessfully challenged by Superintendent George Arthur in 1817, though he did manage to proclaim all unclaimed land to be Crown Land, henceforth to be granted only by the Crown's representative (Bolland and Shoman 1977: 34 – 42).

Prior to emancipation in 1838, the number of 'free people of colour' in Belize had increased substantially until they were almost half of the population, but in addition to the usual forms and processes of discrimination the extraordinary degree of economic monopoly made them almost entirely dependent upon the 'forestocracy.'

After apprenticeship was abolished, the majority of the population remained poor and dependent largely because they were landless.

While the forestocracy were confirmed in their possession of virtually all the accesisble land in Belize, land that they had acquired gratuitously, Crown land was not to be freely granted after 1838 for fear that allowing the ex-slaves to obtain land might 'discourage labour for wages.'

The result of this policy was that no Crown land was sold in the period up to 1855, and by 1868 the total amount sold was said to be 'utterly insignificant.'" – (Ibid., p. 80).

Refusal by the white settlers to give or sell land to blacks had profound implications not only in economic terms; it also profoundly affected the settlement pattern, creating a demographic landscape which reflected these historical patterns. And it explains why there were very few black communities in the rural areas.

They had been denied land and ended up living in urban areas, mostly in Belize Town which later became Belize City.

Freed slaves remained virtual slaves because of a system that was designed to keep them in perpetual bondage even after emancipation. As Bolland states:

"The inability of the ex-slaves to obtain suitable land, combined with the undeveloped internal market system and a method of labour control that combined advance payments and truck practices to create virtual debt servitude, meant that small farming was not a practical means of livelihood. In Belize, therefore, despite the apparently favourable man/land ratio, a peasantry did not develop after Emancipation as it did in Jamaica and British Guiana.

The slaves of Belize had been accustomed to growing provisions such as plantains, rice, and ground foods in temporary provision grounds near the mahogany camps, but this was largely undertaken to supplement their rations.

Such seasonal or shifting cultivation was compatible with the economy of timber extraction – indeed, it is more accurate to say that agriculture was largely restricted to this form by the predominant economy – but it did not encourage the development of a settled agricultural system.

The forest workers, both during slavery and after, had little time or opportunity to devote to farming. Even though the provision grounds were usually on the river banks, the time needed to transport produce to the market in Belize Town and, even more, to return upriver, was generally prohibitive. As a result of all these factors, the growth of rural communities after Emancipation n Belize was severely retarded (Ashcraft 1973: 80 – 85).

There is evidence of maroon communities in Belize during the time of slavery, but they do not appear to have survived. Most Creole villages – as distinct from Maya, Garifuna, and Mestizo communities – were established late in the nineteenth or in the twentieth century." (N.O. Bolland, *Colonialism and Resistance in Belize: Essays in Historical Sociology*, Ibid., pp. 80, 82)

The Creole are associated with urban life more than any other ethnic group or community in Belize because of this historical pattern created and perpetuated by the white settlers who owned the slaves and determined and shaped the fate of the descendants of these African slaves.

Slavery in the settlement of Belize was associated with the extraction of timber because treaties forbade the production of plantation crops. And even if large-scale plantations had been allowed for commercial farming, ex-slaves would not have benefited from this economic activity because of discrimination.

Settlers needed only one or two slaves to cut logwood. But after logwood lost its importance and mahogany became the primary commodity in the forestry industry especially in the last 25 years of the 18th century, the British settlers needed more land for larger-scale operations. And that more slaves to meet the labour requirements of such operations.

Besides those who worked in the forestry industry, there were slaves who worked as domestic servants. There were others who worked as sailors and as blacksmiths. Some even worked as nurses.

The experience of African slaves and their descendants in Belize was different from the experience of other slaves in places such as Jamaica and Trinidad where they worked mostly on the plantations. That was because the economies were set up differently.

But there was no qualitative difference between the two.

It is true that there were no plantations in Belize. Therefore the slaves did not work on any plantation. It was a different economic pattern determined by the forestry industry.

But in spite of all that, slaves in Belize were still oppressed by their masters. Their masters were brutal, subjecting the slaves to "extreme inhumanity," according to one report published in 1820. And there were other documented accounts of such brutality.

This was also clearly demonstrated by the persistent attempts, many of them successful, by a large number of slaves to escape from their masters.

Many of them fled to Yucatán in the 1700s. And in the early 1800s, many African slaves fled to Guatemala. Others went to Honduras, travelling down the coast from Guatemala.

African slaves were not in Belize from the beginning when the Baymen – buccaneers and pirates – first went to the region But they played a very important role in the economic growth of Belize.

The British settlers knew that they desperately needed them especially in the logging industry, the main economic foundation of the colonial settlement when it was first established. And there is no question that logging, which was a thriving business during that period, could not have been run successfully without abundant and free labour provided by African slaves.

But when the logging business began to decline, due to the scarcity of logwood which had been extensively harvested through the decades, the Baymen turned to mahogany and tropical cedar to stay in business.

Another reason why logwood was no longer a major source of income was that prices for this commodity fell in Europe. Other dye products were also developed, replacing the dye from logwood. It no longer became necessary.

But this also caused a lot problems. When the Baymen started cutting down tropical cedar and mahogany trees as a source of income, they ended up going deeper into the forests where the Maya lived. This brought them into direct conflict with the indigenous people who lived in the villages built in the forests.

Great Britain first sent an official representative to the area of Belize in 1786. Before then, the British

31

government did not recognise Belize as a British colony. The government in Britain feared that recognising Belize as its colony would have caused a lot of problems.

The British were reluctant to establish any kind of formal – colonial – government in the area because they did not want to antagonise the Spanish settlers who occupied a bigger area in the region, virtually surrounding what came to be known as the country of Belize.

But such non-intervention by Britain also had serious consequences. It led to the occupation of Belize as a personal fiefdom for the wealthy English and Scottish settlers, but mostly English.

Instead of establishing democratic institutions or enacting fair laws, powerful settlers took matters into their hands and made decisions to protect and promote their own interests to the detriment of the larger community.

They passed their own laws, established their own government, and gained control of the local legislature which no longer remained representative. It came to represent the interests of the few wealthy settlers, while ignoring the interests of the poor and the powerless. They also ended up owning most of the land in the settlement and gained control of the timber trade.

But not everything worked in their favour. There was persistent threat from their rivals, the Spanish rulers who claimed the entire Central America, including Belize, as their own territory. There were also threats from the indigenous people.

Conflict between the indigenous people and the new comers from Europe continued; while the buccaneers were ruthless in their pursuit, determined to continue cutting down tropical cedar and mahogany trees in the forests.

The Maya attacked the British encampments in the forests but without much success, and the area of Belize was on its way to becoming a British colony.

The Spanish settlers who surrounded Belize tried several times to seize the territory. But they were not successful.

Spanish forces launched their final attack on the British settlement in Belize on 10 September 1798. They were equally unsuccessful. The British were able to defend the settlement and neutralised any attempts by the Spanish to seize Belize or dislodge the British settlers from the territory.

In fact, it was a decisive victory for the people of Belize when they defeated a large Spanish fleet at The Battle of St. George's Caye on 10 September 1798. The anniversary of the battle is now a national holiday in Belize.

But the battle was not fought just on the 10th of September.

It was a short military conflict. It lasted for about a week, from 3 September to 10 September, and was fought off the coast of Belize. However, the name of The Battle of St. George's Caye is typically reserved for the final battle which was fought on the 10th.

The invading force came from Mexico. The Spanish invaders wanted to seize Belize from the British settlers. They were met with a smaller force of Baymen, woodcutters living in Belize, who were assisted by their African slaves.

The final battle went on for two-and-a-half hours. The Spanish invaders, ravaged by yellow fever, withdrew and the British settlers declared victory.

The territory that is now Belize had been in dispute since the mid-1750s, claimed by both Spain and Great Britain. Although Spain never occupied the territory, she claimed it as hers like Mexico and Guatemala simply because, geographically, it was part of Central America, sharing borders with both Mexico and Guatemala, as well as Honduras, another Spanish territory to the south.

When British settlers – Baymen – entered the territory in 1638, their intention was to harvest logwood, and later mahogany, and not to create a new country, although some of them may have had colonial ambitions.

But their main interest was to make money by cutting down and selling logwood. And the Spanish – the government of Spain – recognised this commercial activity, but not occupation of the territory by the British. Colonial or not, they wanted them out of there.

Recognition – by both Britain and Spain – of the timber trade conducted by the British settlers in Belize was formalised by the Treaty of Paris signed in 1763.

But the treaty did not clearly demarcate the territory. There were no clearly defined boundaries showing that this was indeed Spanish territory or a Spanish possession with clearly-defined. territorial boundaries.

Also, there were no terms stipulated in the treaty to show or even suggest that Spain itself had well-defined boundaries around the territory that came to be known as British Honduras, and later as Belize.

It was therefore open to more disputes. And hostilities between the two colonial powers continued.

Hostilities between the two countries ended in 1783 with the signing of the Treaty of Versailles which allowed British settlers rights between the Belize and Hondo rivers. This was extended to the Sibun River on terms agreed upon under the Convention of London signed in 1786. And cutting rights were granted to the settlers on the condition that the settlement – founded and established by the British – be recognised as belonging to Spain.

But the Spanish were determined to seize Belize. The British settlers – Baymen – were also determined to defend their settlement. And they got some help, including muskets and ammunition, from the British in Jamaica.

When they engaged the Spanish invaders, the battle became a defining moment in the history of Belize and the entire Central America. And the help of African slaves can not be underestimated. They played a major role in determining the outcome of the battle because of their knowledge of warfare.

The Battle of St. George's Caye was fought at sea but there were also 700 men on land waiting to defend the territory just in case the Spanish force landed ashore.

By September 13, the Spaniards were in full retreat and the British settlers pursued them to push them farther.

Conditions in Belize did not improve much after the battle, but the threat of Spanish attacks on the British settlement decreased significantly.

In the early 1800s, the British government sought greater control over the British settlement in Belize. Britain also told the settlers they would lose the right to govern themselves if they did not observe Britain's instructions to abolish slavery.

Although slavery was abolished in the British Empire in 1838, there was little or no change in working conditions for the freed slaves and labourers in the British settlement in Belize.

African slaves in Belize were highly valued for their ability to harvest timber, especially mahogany which had now become the main commodity after logwood extraction virtually ended.

Soon after, a series of institutions were put in place to ensure the continued presence of a viable labour force. Some of these included greatly restricting the ability of individuals to obtain land, and a debt-peonage system to control the newly "freed" slaves.

Also the freed slaves had nowhere to go. And the settlement was fully controlled by whites. Black people therefore had no choice but to continue working for whites even when they were free.

In 1836, after the emancipation of Belize from Spanish rule, the British claimed the right to administer the region as a colony.

In 1862, Great Britain formally declared it a British crown colony and named it British Honduras. The colony was headed by a lieutenant governor who was subordinate to the governor of Jamaica.

About three years earlier in 1859, Britain and Guatemala signed the Anglo-Guatemalan Treaty which established the western boundary – that exists today – between Belize and Guatemala. The treaty temporarily settled the question of Guatemala's claim on Belize; a dispute that continues today.

As a colony, Belize began to attract British investors. Among the British firms that dominated the colony in the late 1800s was the Belize Estate and Produce Company which eventually acquired half of all the privately-held land in the colony.

But while all these changes were taking place, mistreatment of the Garifuna – and of the former slaves – continued. Nothing had changed for them. They remained subordinate to the British settlers and did not have equal rights which were taken for granted by whites in British Honduras (Belize).

In 1872, The Crown Lands Ordinance was passed, establishing restrictions for the Garifuna and for the Maya. The British prevented both groups from owning land and treated them as a source of cheap labour. It amounted to virtual slavery.

However, resistance by the Maya continued until the 1870s, more than a decade after the colony of British Honduras had been established.

The conflict between the two started long before then because of British encroachment on Mayan territory as the British consolidated their settlement and pushed deeper into the interior in search of mahogany.

The Maya had some success against the British in some of these encounters. But in most cases, the British won.

One of the most notable successes by the Maya was in 1866 when they defeated a detachment of British troops sent to San Pedro. Earlier in the same year, a group of the Maya attacked a mahogany camp on the Bravo River. Conflicts between the two were far from over, although they were to end only a few years later.

Early in 1867, British troops marched into areas in which the Maya had settled and destroyed villages in an attempt to drive them out. The expelled Mayans returned and occupied the town of Corozal in the western part of British Honduras in April 1870.

An unsuccessful attack by the Mayans on Orange Walk – also in western British Honduras – in 1872 was the last serious attack on the British colony of Honduras.

Also, other developments took place through the years and played a major role in shaping and reshaping the demographic and cultural identity of British Honduras. The indigenous people were one of the major forces of change especially in the demographic transformation of the colony.

In the 1880s and 1890s, two major groups of the Maya fled from forced labour under Spanish rule in Guatemala and settled in several villages in southern British Honduras.

They became an integral part of British Honduras, ruled by indirect rule, a system of government that was perfected by the British in other parts of their colonial empire including Africa where the colonial rulers used local rulers including chiefs to control the indigenous people.

But because the Maya lived in remote, isolated areas in the southern part of British Honduras, they did not become fully integrated into the colony as other people did. In fact, their fellow indigenes in the northern part of British Honduras became more integrated into the colonial society although they still retained their traditional ways and their cultural identity. Northern British Honduras became a stronghold of Mestizo culture.

By the end of the 1800s, the ethnic configuration of British Honduras – that remained largely intact throughout the 20th century – was already in place. It also had a religious dimension.

The ethnic pattern consisted of Protestants, mainly of African descent, who spoke either English or Creole and lived in Belize Town; the Roman Catholic Mayans and Mestizos who spoke Spanish and who lived mainly in the northern and western parts of the colony; and the Roman Catholic Garifuna who spoke English, Spanish, or Garifuna and who settled on the southern coast.

But threat from the Maya was not completely over. The people who lived in the town of Belize, especially the merchants, felt that they were relatively secure from attacks by these indigenous people. They did not even want to contribute towards the protection of mahogany camps in the interior which were susceptible to Mayan attacks. But the landowners felt differently. They felt that they should not be required to pay taxes on lands which did not get adequate protection.

It was a conflict of interest and it led to a stalemate. The colonial Legislative Assembly of British Honduras failed to authorise the raising of sufficient revenue for the colony, especially for its protection.

The political rulers of the colony now had only one option left. They relinquished power and asked for the establishment of direct British rule in return for greater security of the crown colony.

It was a fundamental change in the way this British territory had been administered.

For 50 years, power had been in the hands of rich settlers who owned most of the land and controlled the economy of the territory. Now power had shifted from the old settler oligarchy to the colonial office in London and to the directors of British companies who had a lot of control over the economy of this British colonial outpost in Central America.

And there was no question that the indigenous people had lost. They were no match for their conquerors from Europe. And logging companies continued to displace Mayan villages deep in the forests in this British colony until the 1950s.

After the colony was established in 1862, several constitutional changes were introduced through the decades to expand representative government.

But there was also the role of powerful economic interests which could not be disregarded in the evolution of this colony including its economic growth.

One of those powerful economic interests was the forestry industry.

The forestry industry's control of land and its influence in colonial decision-making slowed the development of agriculture and the diversification of the economy. Although British Honduras had vast areas of sparsely populated, unused land, landownership was controlled by a small European monopoly, thwarting the evolution of a Creole landowning class from the African former slaves.

It was blatant discrimination. Even the end of slavery had not radically transformed the lives of former slaves.

Landownership became even more consolidated during the economic depression of the mid-1800s. And the depression had a profound impact on the colony and ts future.

Major results of the depression included the decline of the old settler class, the increasing consolidation of capital, and the intensification of British landownership.

The British Honduras Company, later renamed the Belize Estate and Produce Company, emerged as the predominant landowner. It had about half of all the privately-held land in the colony. And the company became the dominant force in British Honduras's political and economic life for more than a century.

Financial moghuls not only controlled the levers of power; they also transformed the political and economic landscape of British Honduras as never before. They had all the money in their hands.

This concentration and centralisation of capital meant that the direction of the colony's economy was henceforth determined largely in London, the financial centre of the British empire. It also signaled the eclipse of the old settler elite in British Honduras.

By about 1890, most commerce in British Honduras was in the hands of a clique of Scottish and German merchants. Most of them were newcomers.

The European minority exercised great influence in the colony's politics partly because they were guaranteed representation in the colonial Legislative Council all of whose members were appointed. Not one was elected by the people. In 1892, the governor appointed several Creole members, but whites remained the majority in this legislative chamber.

However, Creoles gradually gained influence through the years, although they were still eclipsed by whites.

In 1927, Creole merchants and professionals replaced the representatives of British landowners on the Legislative Council, except for the manager of the Belize Estate and Produce Company.

The participation of Creoles in the political process was a fundamental change in the British colony. And it signalled the beginning of other changes which would later radically transform the society especially in terms of power. And the colony functioned fairly well until the Great Depression came.

The economy of British Honduras almost collapsed during the Great Depression in the 1930s because of the low demand for timber in Britain. Also, there was very high unemployment during the Depression, compounded by the damage caused by a devastating hurricane which hit British Honduras in 1931.

There were also widespread perceptions among the people that the government did not want to help them during the crisis. This was compounded by the colonial government's refusal to legalise labour unions and introduce minimum wage.

The Great Depression of the 1930s also had a profound

impact on British Honduras in other ways.

It destroyed the economy. Many jobs were lost and and unemployment rose sharply.

The problem was compounded by a natural disaster of great proportions. The country was hit by a hurricane on10 September 1931. it was the worst in the nation's recent history and destroyed Belize Town. More than 1,000 people were killed.

To make things worse, response to the disaster was slow and inadequate. The people in the colony expected help from Britain. They did not get it, at least not in the amount they expected. Instead, the British government took advantage of the situation to expand its authority over the colony. It imposed tighter control on the colony and gave the governor more power to enact laws in emergency situations.

Those were hard times for the colony and the Belize Estate and Produce Company survived the depression only because of its special connections in British Honduras and London.

As the depression continued, conditions also continued to get worse, especially for the poor.

Workers in mahogany camps were treated almost like slaves. To add insult to injury, most of the workers in those camps were black, descendants of slaves, or indigenous people who had already lost their land to the European settlers.

There was even a law governing labour contracts, passed years earlier in 1883, which made it illegal and a criminal offence for a labourer to break a contract with his or her employer. In such a racially stratified society, it was obvious the law targeted blacks and other non-whites.

The pain and suffering during the Great Depression was hard enough without inflicting more pain on the poor by enforcing such an unjust law. It was a draconian law enforced during the worst of times.

In 1931 the governor of British Honduras   rejected

proposals to legalise trade unions and introduce minimum wage and sickness insurance. But the people, mostly poor, did not give up.

In 1934 they responded with a series of demonstrations, strikes, petitions and riots which marked the beginning of modern politics and the independence movement in British Honduras. It was a turning point in the history of the colony.

The defiance campaigns and riots fuelled the independence struggle which later evolved into a well-organised independence movement across the country.

In an attempt to defuse tensions and calm down the people, the colonial government repealed criminal penalties for workers who broke their labour contracts and granted workers the right to join unions.

Riots, strikes, and rebellions had occurred before, but the events of the 1930s had gone much further. They were modern labour disturbances in the sense that they gave rise to organisations which were able to articulate well-defined industrial and political goals and grievances as never before.

Economic conditions improved during World War II when many men joined the armed forces or engaged in other activities which contributed labour to the war effort; a situation similar to what happened in the United States during the same period when the unemployment rate was lowest in 1944 because many people found jobs which supported the war.

But after the war, the economy of British Honduras suffered again, causing more problems including social unrest.

The leaders of the labour oganisations sharply criticised the governor and his colleagues as well as the rich merchants, including the Belize Estate and Produce Company, for their mistreatment of the workers. They pointed to the injustices and forcefully articulated the workers' demands in political and moral terms.

And there was a corresponding rise in the political consciousness of the people, especially no-whites, as the injustices continued. Former Africans slaves, the indigenous people and others were the primary victims of the injustices being perpetrated against the poor and the weak most of whom were non-white.

All this contributed to the emergence of a new awareness which led to the development of nationalist sentiments and demands for democracy.

To avoid civil unrest, the governor acceded to some of the demands by the workers. The immediate result was the creation of relief work. It was a tactical move by the governor and a partial victory for the people but it helped defuse tensions.

The workers continued to press their demands. Their greatest achievements were labour reforms which were passed between 1941 and 1943.

Trade unions were legalised in 1941. And in 1943, a law was passed which clearly stated that it was no longer illegal for workers to break contracts. The new law removed breach-of-labor-contract from the criminal code. It was a major achievement by poor and ordinary people in their quest for justice.

It was in the same year, 1943, that the General Workers Union (GWU), formerly known as the Workers and Tradesmen's Union, was registered. And it played a major role in the political transformation of the country.

The union quickly expanded into a nationwide organisation and provided crucial support for the nationalist movement which gained momentum after a major political party, the People's Union Party (PUP), was formed in 1950.

The 1940s was one of the most important decades in the history of British Honduras. It marked the beginning of fundamental change in the political life of the country, with labour leaders and other people pushing for democratic rights including universal suffrage.

Britain's decision to devalue the British Honduras dollar in 1949 worsened economic conditions and led to the creation of the People's Committee which demanded independence.

The People's Committee formed the nucleus of the independence movement and was later transformed into a political party, the People's United Party (PUP), which sought constitutional reforms that would expand voting rights to all adults.

A turning point took place in December 1949 when the governor of British Honduras devalued the currency without the approval of the Legislative Council which was supposed to represent the people. It was a unilateral decision by the governor. And it had major implications across the country.

It showed that the colonial rulers had extensive powers which they could exercise at will even if what they did was against the wishes of the majority of the people in British Honduras. It also showed that the colonial legislature which was supposed to represent the people had very little power and leverage in the conduct of national affairs. It was the governor and his colleagues who had all the power, and they did not represent the people of British Honduras.

All this helped fuel the independence movement, with the governor's decision to devalue the British Honduras dollar, against the wishes of the Legislative Council, being the most prominent factor which pushed nationalists to the extreme. They felt, and rightly so, that the people were being ignored and colonial rule was undemocratic. It was time for change.

The devaluation of the currency also angered labour organisations because it protected the interests of the big transnational companies while forcing the poor and working-class people to pay higher prices for the items they bought including basic necessities such as food.

The governor's decision therefore had unintended

consequences. It became a rallying cry for the people and it united labour leaders, political activists and Creole middle class members in a broad coalition of interests to demand concessions from the colonial rulers and agitate for independence.

The devaluation of the currency was a blessing to the colonised people of British Honduras. It galvanised them into action as never before.

On the same night that the British governor announced devaluation of the currency, nationalists also made an important decision.

They formed the People's Committee, the same night. And the independence movement which had been growing gradually through the decade during the 1940s now became a force to be reckoned with in national politics and in the life of the country as a whole. It was the beginning of the end of colonial rule in British Honduras.

The People's Committee was dissolved in September 1950 and was replaced by the People's United Party (PUP), a national movement demanding independence.

The PUP went into action and, from 1950 to 1954, did a lot of grass-root work mobilising the people across the country in pursuit of its agenda for independence. Its activists forcefully articulated its demands and the message resonated well among the people.

High on the agenda was constitutional reforms. But the People's United Party had other important items on the agenda including currency devaluation which helped galvanise the independence movement.

Also on the agenda was the proposed West Indian Federation.

The nationalists in British Honduras wanted their country to join the federation after independence because of its historical ties to the island nations of the Caribbean which were also British colonies and had large populations of people of African origin. All of them were also linked by a common history of slavery besides their common

African heritage.

But more than anything else during that time was the demand for constitutional reforms which would pave the way towards full independence. Constitutional reforms which started in 1954 led to a new constitution 10 years later.

Therefore, the People's United Party concentrated on agitating for constitutional reforms including universal adult suffrage without a literacy test; an all-elected Legislative Council; an Executive Council chosen by the leader of the majority party in the legislature; the introduction of a ministerial system; and the abolition of the governor's reserve powers.

In short, the PUP pushed for representative and responsible government.

The colonial rulers were not amused by all this. Alarmed by the growing support for the PUP across the country, they retaliated by attacking two of the party's main public platforms: the Belize City Council and the PUP itself.

But the independence movement weathered the storm. The People's United Party (PUP) had already become a powerful political force and nothing was going to stop it in its pursuit of total independence.

All attempts by the colonial rulers to discredit the PUP failed.

The main test came in April 1954 when voters went to the polls. It was the first election under universal literate adult suffrage. And the main issue was clearly colonialism. A vote for the PUP was a vote for self-government.

Almost 70 per cent of the electorate voted. The PUP won 66.3 per cent of the vote. It also won 8 of the 9 elected seats in the new Legislative Assembly.

Further constitutional reforms were clearly on the agenda. Change was irreversible. Independence loomed on the horizon.

But there were obstacles on the road to independence.

One was, until the early 1960s, the reluctance by Britain to allow the people of British Honduras to govern themselves.

The other one was Guatemala's total refusal to accept British Honduras as a separate territorial entity with the right to exist as a sovereign nation.

Guatemala had always claimed that the entire territory of British Honduras belonged to Guatemala and had even repeatedly threatened to use force to annex the territory. Only Britain's military might discouraged Guatemala from launching a full-scale offensive to take over British Honduras.

However, by 1961, Britain relented – although grudgingly – to let the colony become independent. Agitation for independence was unstoppable.

Negotiations between Britain and Guatemala over the disputed territory started again in 1961, but the elected representatives of British Honduras had no voice in these talks.

The leader of the nationalist movement, George Cadle Price, rejected an offer by Guatemala to make British Honduras an "associated state" of Guatemala. He made it clear that he wanted full independence.

In 1963 Guatemala stopped the negotiations and ended diplomatic relations with Britain.

And in January 1964, British Honduras won full internal self-government under a ministerial system. The head of the PUP, George Cadle Price, became the colony's prime minister.

But Britain remained in control in a number of critical areas. The colonial power controlled defence. It also controlled foreign affairs, internal security and the civil service since the country had not yet attained full independence.

The dispute with Guatemala also remained a major issue. Talks between Guatemala and British Honduras on the border dispute went on intermittently and stopped abruptly during the late 1960s and early 1970s.

But the failure of those negotiations did not stop the quest for independence. The nationalist leaders in the colony continued to carry on the struggle and the official name of the territory was changed from British Honduras to Belize in June 1973 in anticipation of full independence.

Still, progress towards independence was not smooth. Guatemala's claim to sovereignty over the territory of Belize threatened to slow down the nationalist movement even if it could not stop it in its quest for full sovereign status.

By 1975, the governments of British Honduras and Britain, frustrated in their dealings with the military-dominated regimes of Guatemala, agreed on a new strategy that would take the case for Belize's self-determination to various international forums.

The government of British Honduras felt that by taking its case to the international arena and gaining support around the world, including support from the United Nations (UN) for its status as a separate territorial entity with the right to self-determination, it could strengthen its position, weaken Guatemala's claims, and make it harder for Britain to make any concessions to Guatemala which continued to claim the entire colonial territory as part of Guatemala.

The nationalist leaders of British Honduras argued that Guatemala was trying to frustrate their country's legitimate aspirations to self-determination.

They also argued that Guatemala was advancing an illegitimate claim and disguising its own colonial ambitions by trying to present the dispute as an effort to reclaim its territory lost to a colonial power: Britain.

Between 1975 and 1981, the leaders of British Honduras presented their case for independence at a number of international forums.

They argued their case at a number of conferences

attended by the heads of state and government at the Commonwealth which is made up of former British colonies. They also presented their case at a conference of ministers of the Nonaligned Movement and at UN meetings.

Initially, Latin American governments supported Guatemala's claim. But that changed when, between 1975 and 1979, British Honduras won the support of Cuba, Mexico, Panama, and Nicaragua.

Finally, in November 1980, with Guatemala completely isolated, the UN passed a resolution that demanded independence for British Honduras.

A last attempt was made to reach an agreement with Guatemala before the colony's independence. But the colony's representatives to the talks made no concessions and a proposal called the Heads of Agreement was reached on 11 March 1981.

However, when conservative political forces in Guatemala denounced Guatemalan proponents of this agreement as sellouts, the Guatemalan government refused to ratify the agreement and withdrew from the negotiations.

Groups in British Honduras which were opposed to any kind of compromise with Guatemala engaged in violent demonstrations against the Heads of Agreement and a state of emergency was declared. But they did not come up with any meaningful proposal to end the dispute with Guatemala in a peaceful way.

One one thing remained clear: independence for British Honduras as soon as possible. And it finally came.

British Honduras attained sovereign status on 21 September 1981 without reaching an agreement with Guatemala on the territorial dispute. And Guatemala refused to recognise Belize as an independent nation.

About 1,500 British troops remained to protect Belize from a possible Guatemalan invasion.

George Cadle Price became the country's first prime

minister. He served as prime minister and minister of foreign affairs from 1981 to 1984, and again as prime minister from 1989 to 1993.

Together with Monrad Metzgen, he was one of the main leaders of the independence movement in British Honduras. He was also a co-founder of the People's United (PUP) Party which led the struggle for independence. He led the party for 40 years.

There was also a change in Belize's relations with Guatemala. In 1992, the president of Guatemala formally recognized Belize's independence.

And in the following year, the United Kingdom announced that it would end its military involvement – in its former colony – whose primary purpose was to protect Belize from Guatemala's territorial ambitions.

All British soldiers were withdrawn in 1994, apart from a small contingent of troops who remained to train Belizean troops.

The withdrawal of British troops from Belize also signalled an end to the territorial dispute with Guatemala. There would have been no need for such military presence, to guarantee security, if there was no threat to Belize's territorial integrity.

But the dispute was never fully resolved in spite of what may be described as peace between the two countries.

In 1993, the prime minister of Belize, Manuel Esquivel, who was also the leader of the United Democratic Party (UDP), announced the suspension of a pact reached with Guatemala during the tenure of Prime Minister George Price, claiming that his predecessor had made too many concessions in order to gain Guatemala's recognition of Belize's independence and territorial integrity.

The pact signed by his predecessor would have resolved a 130 year-old border dispute between the two countries. It did not, especially after being renounced in

1993 by the government of Belize.

The pact also did not gain full acceptance in Guatemala. There were, and still there are, elements in Guatemala's leadership who maintain that Belize is part of Guatemala and will always be.

Border tensions between the two countries continued into the early 2000s, although the two neighbours cooperated in other areas of mutual interest.

But tensions are bound to continue and may even erupt into hostilities in the future because of Guatemala's claims.

Throughout Belize's history, Guatemala has claimed ownership of all or part of the territory of this small Central American nation. This claim is occasionally reflected in Guatemalan maps showing Belize as Guatemala's twenty-third province, and not as a separate independent country as it is shown in other maps around the world.

The border dispute remains unresolved and quite contentious and has at various times required intervention and mediation by other countries and international organisations including the United Kingdom, the Caribbean Community heads of government, the Organisation of American States (OAS), the United States, and the UN.

A British garrison has remained in Belize at the request of the Belizean government since independence because of that.

Without guarantee of security by the United Kingdom, Belize faces the prospect of an invasion by Guatemala.

In a tragic way, Belize's independence is real only because it is guaranteed by its former colonial master, the United Kingdom; a contradiction hard for any weak country to resolve.

It's a harsh reality to live with, especially when you claim to be independent, yet you can not even defend yourself or guarantee your independence.

Belize also continues to be a nation of ethnic and racial diversity, although problems of racial inequality and other injustices continue to exist. Also, race relations are not as good as some people claim. And there are many cases to illustrate this point.

Mestizos are derisively described by some Belizeans as "aliens"even by descendants of African slaves such as Kriols and and Garifunas who should know better because of their history of suffering as victims of slavery and racial injustice.

Although Mestizos are Belizeans, they are told they are not an integral part of the Belizian nation. Mestizos are also – because of their Spanish ancestry – accused of being sympathetic to Guatemala which wants to annex Belize.

Descendants of the Maya, the most disadvantaged group, are also not considered by some of their fellow countrymen to be true Belizeans. They are, instead, told that they belong to other parts of Central America.

And blacks, although they have always been an integral part of Belize from the beginning and even at one time – as early as 1800 – outnumbered whites 4 to 1, still carry the stigma of slavery which is associated with racial inferiority although many of them have been prominent in many areas of national life including leadership.

Also, dark skin is still seen as a badge of inferiority and ugliness. Even the fact that many blacks have risen to positions of prominence in national life including academia has not changed this perception and stereotype. They are still considered by many non-blacks to be the most inferior and least intelligent people on earth.

And it was not until February 2008 that a black, Dean Oliver Barrow, the leader of the United Democratic Party (UDP), rose to the highest office in the land and became prime minister. He became the first black to serve in that position.

He once served as deputy prime minister and as

minister of foreign affairs from 1993 to 1998 when his party was in power. And he became the leader of the opposition from 1998 and served in that capacity until February 2008 when the UDP won the election, thrusting him into national leadership.

Yet in spite of all those problems, Belize does not have the kind of inter-ethnic and racial strife that has wreaked havoc in many countries around the world, even if it's not a veritable paradise in the tropics. As Professor Irma McClaurin, who became the first African American to get tenure in the department of anthropology at the University of Florida in 1999, states in her book *Women of Belize: Gender and Change in Central America*:

"It would be untrue to paint a portrait of Belize as a country completely without conflict.

There are ethnic tensions that can be traced to colonial policies and practices; moreover, recent competition over jobs and other strategic resources has th potential to pit ethnic groups against one another in the future as the population struggles to survive in an atmosphere of shrinking natural resources and rising costs.

A Mosaic: 'Many Cultures, One Nation'

Perhaps the most interesting aspect of Belize is its people. As one moves about the country, ethnicity is real and palpable.

In many respects an infant among independent nations, Belize offers a lesson to the giants that grapple with questions of cultural tolerance, equality, and ethnic civility. Though not without internal problems and operational ethnic boundaries and tensions, the country still lacks the ethnic turmoil of a Guyana or a Trinidad.

Nor does the country exemplify either the structural dimensions of segregation and institutional racism that characterize the United States or the intense color caste system of Jamaica.

Belize might be called truly 'multicultural.' The government actively seeks to construct a national identity that deemphasizes ethnic differences and builds on common national interests. Its efforts are captured in a former slogan of the People's United Party, 'We all de one,' and in the United Democratic Party's more recent rallying cry, 'Many cultures, one nation.'

One major reason for Belize's lack of stressed ethnic relations is spatial. Fredrik Barth has argued that where ethnic groups can maintain distances that allow them to create their own niches, diminishing competition for strategic resources, ethnic conflicts are minimal.

Spatial circumstances can be cited to explain why Belize has not experienced the extreme ethnic tensions that characterize social relations in some of the surrounding Central American countries or among some of its Caribbean neighbors.

The two largest ethnic groups – Mestizos and Creoles – in Belize are geographically dispersed.

Mestizos live in those areas of the country bordering Mexico and Guatemala; Creoles dominate Belize City. Moreover, neither group can claim to be the 'original' Belizeans, since nearly all of the country's population came from somewhere else." – (Irma McClaurin, *Women of Belize: Gender and Change in Central America*, Newark, New Jersey: Rutgers University, 1 August 1996, pp. 29 – 30).

Different origins also sustain and reinforce ethnic distinctions and identities especially in societies where assimilation or integration has not been fully achieved. People of different origins tend to maintain ties with their own kind and with their original homelands even if only in the cultural realm by retaining and transmitting to the younger generations values, customs and traditions from the old country.

That has not been quite the case in Belize where descendants of African slaves lost their African cultures during slavery. But mere identification with Africa is enough to sustain a spirit of unique identity in a society which is composed of different ethnic, racial and cultural groups with different origins. And as McClaurin states:

"The ancestors of most Belizeans arrived by force from Africa and the West Indies as slaves, others came from India as indentured laborers, and still others first crossed over the borders of Belize from the Yucatan to escape the bloody turmoil during the Guerras de Casta (Caste Wars).

Even many of the present-day Maya, who are the 'original' people of the area according to archaeologists, also immigrated.

Travel writers and historians both assert that only a small segment of the Maya population now living in Belize can claim to be direct descendants of the people who built the ruins that so delight archaeologists and attest to the presence of a highly developed Maya civilization at one time.

The majority of those living in Belize today are believed to be descendants of Maya from adjacent empires who fled from the Yucatan in the nineteenth century and of later groups of Mopan and Kekchi Maya in the south of Belize who came during the late nineteenth century to escape forced labor plantations in their native Guatemala. While to the outside eyes these groups are all Maya – that is, a homogeneous group – among themselves they separated by language – Yucateco, Mopanero, and Kekchi – and different interests.

Ethnic boundaries do exist in Belize among the various groups, but people who reside in close proximity interact without enmity.

The consequences for marrying outside the group are generally not severe, though stories of violence against one party of an interethnic relationship do surface." – (Ibid., p. 30).

There is no question that the issue of ethnicity is of some concern even in Belize where inter-ethnic relations are relatively harmonious.

And it is a complex phenomenon in the Belizean context because of the way the society has evolved through the years, sometimes blurring ethnic distinctions, with ethnic identity assuming a cultural dimension in sharp contrast with racial identity. This complexity plays a major role in defining and shaping inter-ethnic relations in Belize.

Also, as in any other country in the world, ethnic identity is a fact of life in Belize, sometimes leading to tensions. This has been clearly demonstrated in recent years, a development attributed to a number of factors. As Professor Anne Sutherland of the University of California-Riverside states in her book *The Making of Belize: Globalization in The Margins*:

"Some Belizean Creole intellectuals and leaders, for example, are trying to raise consciousness of and pride in the African roots of Creoles and Garifuna. In addition, both the Garifuna and the Maya have their own cultural associations to revitalize their indigenous roots....

There is an increase in the rhetoric of ethnicity in Belize and its use by Belizeans to describe themselves. Such rhetoric can be heard both in the streets and in private conversation: it has existed for some time, making it hard to measure just how much it has increased over time.

However, in the last few years, Belizean politicians have become more vocal about expressing social issues in terms of ethnicity. Furthermore, newspapers regularly feature articles, letters, and op-ed pieces expressing concern about ethnic divisiveness and negative racial stereotypes among Belizeans. Many of these writings are responses to Amandala's openly Afrocentric position – a position that most Belizeans do not share." – (Anne Sutherland, *The Making of Belize: Globalization in The Margins*, New York: Bergin & Garvey, 30 July 1998, pp. 80, 81 – 82).

The Afrocentric position is irrelevant, and divisive, in the larger Belizean context because Belize is not a predominantly black nation.

Even in the Creole community itself, it may be relevant only to a minority group since the majority of Creoles and other people of African descent don't share its strident rhetoric and militant message which they consider to be divisive in a multiracial and multicultural society.

Yet it has a powerful message which resonates well among its adherents even if they are a minority. But they do tap into the fear that may be prevalent among a significant number of blacks who feel that they are being marginalised.

Many people of African descent around the world – including those in Belize – are also aware of their position as members of what may be the most despised race on earth, based on historical experience.

All that is harnessed by a number of blacks in Belize in an attempt to mobilise other blacks into a potent political force whose message and mission is defined by their ethnic identity and interests.

However, this ethnic consciousness is not peculiarly black. It's common among other groups even though it may be more pronounced among Belizeans of African descent who are members of the Creole and Garifuna communities. And as Sutherland states:

"It may be too soon to know how ethnic divisiveness will develop, but certain events stand out as markers of its increase.

First, Belize, as one of the last British colonies to gain independence, has become a nation in which the idea of a specifically Belizean national – as opposed to colonial – identity has taken shape only since the early 1980s.

Consciousness of Belizean identity, of course, is not new and was a feature of Belize before independence. What does represent a more recent change is the convergence of the post-independence political development of Belize and things Belizean with the end of the Cold War global emphasis on ethnicity as identity.

For example, in an article titled 'Is There A Future for Africanness in Belize?' Joseph Palacio argues that in Belize, cultural identity has been more important than skin color:

'The Belize case introduces the concept of cultural segmentation as overriding identity among peoples sharing black skin colour. Or, in other words, two persons may be black but they relate primarily to their distinct ethnic culture and not their colour' (1996, 36).

Palacio goes on to say that this is a 'problem' because it has led to a rejection of Africa, even though the foundation of Belizean culture, was African, and what is needed is a renewed identification with Africa, a revitalization of African elements in Belizean culture, and a privileged status for immigrants of African descent:

'Very few people pay tribute to the fact that it was the desire of persons of African ancestry for freedom that became a founding stone for what would eventually become the nation state of Belize....With such a significant lead, how has Africanness eroded within a period of a little more than two hundred years?....

What the Garifuna and Creole have not fully realized is that they are products of a British colonial system that inflicted on them the original sin of hating blackness and the source of that blackness, mother Africa....

At the community level the responsibility lies for all peoples of African ancestry to heal the cultural divide that has separated them. The principal actors are the Garifuna and the Creole. The aim would be to identify and retrieve the common African elements that they share in language, food, traditional medicine, religious beliefs, aesthetic culture, abiding sense of kinship, etc.

Closely related would be to extend to Africans and West Indians some sort of preferred immigrant status that Latinos have taken for granted during the past three decades.' (1996, 34, 35, 44)

One of the difficulties of appealing to primordialism in race issues in a multicultural society is deciding which identity to consider primary.

Thus, in spite of calls for Creole/Garifuna unity as African brothers, the Garifuna, as often as not, are concerned with their indigenous roots and identity more than with their African ancestry (Kearns 1983; Foster 1986). According to Godsman Ellis, the founder of the Garifuna Cultural Council, the Garifuna see themselves as an oppressed indigenous group." – (Anne Sutherland, *The Making of Belize: Globalization in The Margins*, ibid., pp. 82 – 83).

The division, differences and mistrust which exist between the Creole and Garifuna communities who, in some respects, are supposed to share a common African identity, clearly show the complex nature of the phenomenon of ethnicity in the Belizean context.

Here are two communities which are supposed to have a common ancestry, a common experience, and a common destiny. Yet they see themselves as different from each other in spite of the rhetoric from some of their leaders advocating solidarity.

Compounding the problem is the mistreatment of the Garifuna by the Creole, an experience which has become an integral part of Garifuna history and that is invoked by many Garifunas to reinforce their identity as a separate group different from the Creole.

Some of the Garifuna may use this history of suffering at the hands of fellow "blacks" – not all Creoles are really black – merely as a clarion call for solidarity among their people. But, inadvertently or not, it also reinforces the belief that they are different from the Creole as a people in spite of their common African heritage and history of slavery:

"Furthermore, the Garifuna – primarily located in

59

Dandriga and Punta Gorda – have not forgotten their not-too-distant treatment by Creoles as social and political inferiors, an attitude fueled by the British, who portrayed the Garifuna as cannibals and kept the two black groups separated by making it necessary for the Garifuna to obtain permits to travel from Dandriga to Belize City.

It is not surprising that the Garifuna have thus developed a strong cultural resurgence and political action movement to elevate their status as an indigenous, rather than an African, people.

Cultural pride among the Garifuna has been heightened b the Garifuna Cultural Council, as manifested in the resurgence of Punta Rock, Garifuna dances, Settlement Day celebrations on November 19, and the effort to revive traditions such as language (Carib/Arawak), rituals, foods, the crafts, most of which are based on indigenous identity (Haug and Haug 1994, 8).

The entire Garifuna nation from Nicaragua, Honduras, and Belize has become linked on the Internet, and they jointly celebrated their bicentennial on April 12, 1997, marking 200 years since leaving St. Vincent." – (Ibid., p. 83).

Ethnicity has also been a factor in politics, although experience has at the same time shown that voters have been able to transcend ethnicity and have voted for candidates outside their ethnic communities.

Still, ethnic loyalty and solidarity is a factor to be reckoned with, especially when some communities feel that they are being ignored or marginalised. As Sutherland goes on to state in her book *The Making of Belize*:

"This recent resurgence of ethnic and cultural identity issues has spilled over into the politics of the two parties – UDP and PUP – that alternately hold power in Belize.

In contrast with the colonial period, in which power was controlled by the British government and the British-appointed local elites, mostly Creoles, today the two Belizean political parties compete for votes partly – but increasingly – by appealing to specific ethnic groups. Many politicians are concerned about ethnicization of the parties, conscious of the inherent dangers in the increase of such cleavages." – (Ibid., pp. 82 – 83).

So, while the ethnic configuration of Belize may reflect a harmonious whole, there is also the perception and the reality that in every group, there is a consciousness of "who and what we are" even if this does not necessarily lead to hostility towards other groups with whom they collectively constitute the nation of Belize.

Ethnic interests have now become a factor in national politics – in fact they always have been although in latent form in many cases – but not to the extent that they threaten national unity.

However, ethnic solidarity may cause some problems in the future if it is promoted at the expense of other groups, as it indeed is, sometimes. Not everybody believes that the interests of the nation are paramount.

But even among those who believe that the interests of the nation should take precedence over group interests, there is a level of ethnic and cultural consciousness that can not be ignored. And it goes to the core of the problem involving conflicting interests between the various groups which collectively constitute the nation of Belize.

There is the question of survival including economic security.

When members of one group feel threatened by another group, or by other groups, in one way or another, there is a tendency to close ranks for their survival. It's a siege mentality which is encouraged even when there is no real threat.

But even when the threat is more apparent than real, the people who feel threatened or victimized or marginalised feel the same way as if they were in real danger.

When this fortress mentality takes over, the level of ethnic or group consciousness and solidarity also increases sharply.

And when there is clear evidence that a group that once had a dominant position in society has lost that position, group consciousness not only increases; it can also lead to hostility towards others, especially those who are perceived to be their biggest competitors.

This happened in Belize when the Creole community lost its position as the largest ethnic and cultural group in the country after immigrants from other countries of Central America entered Belize in the 1980s and 1990s in very large numbers.

Besides conflicts in their countries, these immigrants were also economic refugees who chose to live in Belize where wages were much higher than they were in their home countries.

Economically, Belize is more developed than all the other countries in Central America, perhaps with the exception of Costa Rica in some areas. And the Central American immigrants came from countries where wages were at least half the wages in Belize. So, to them, life in Belize was some kind of paradise.

This has fuelled tension because native Belizeans complain that the immigrants lower wages. Employers are willing to hire them for their cheap labour, making it very difficult for Belizeans to get the same kind of jobs at higher wages.

The tension has also led to stereotypes, with many native Belizeans such as Creoles calling them names including racial slurs similar to what desperate illegal immigrants from Mexico experience in the United States. They are called "wetbacks" – for swimming across the Rio Grande to get into the United States – and other names including "tacos" and "enchiladas."

Some have even been attacked physically, a form of

ethnic intimidation which can lead to death, even though Belize tries to project itself as a country where ethnic harmony is the norm rather than the exception.

Another source of tension is acculturation. Most immigrants send their children to English schools so that they can learn the country's main language and become integrated into the society, but *not* to stay in Belize permanently. They want the children to immigrate to the United States eventually.

When native Belizeans find that out, they become even more hostile towards the immigrants whom they already don't see as Belizeans. They see them as opportunists who simply want to use Belize for their own benefit, including getting jobs and preparing their children, at Belize's expense, to immigrate to the United States.

That's one of the areas of ethnic tensions where Belizeans of different ethno-cultural groups agree on the menace of Central American immigrants whom they see as nothing but economic refugees and opportunists thriving at Belize's expense.

Among Belizeans themselves – including the new immigrants from the Central American countries – ethnic consciousness is sharpened for other reasons as well.

Ethnic consciousness is also very strong as a matter of pride even when members of a group don't feel threatened. All groups in Belize are proud of their heritage. And no amount of nationalist sentiment is going to overcome or replace that.

Some of the most nationalist-minded people in Belize – or anywhere else in the world – are also some of the most ethnically conscious. Again, the Creole provide a good example in the case of Belize.

It was the Creole who led the independence movement in British Honduras, creating a sense of national consciousness that did not exist before. This consciousness took shape when the struggle for independence gained momentum across the country especially since the 1950s.

Yet it was the Creole themselves who also remained as some of the most ethnically conscious people in Belize even after the country won independence about 30 years later.

They were even accused of practising discrimination against other groups in terms of employment since they dominated the civil service and other areas of national life to the "detriment" of non-Creoles; the Garifuna, to whom they're closely related in terms of African roots, are prominent in the educational field. But the two groups are not as close as they could be. Even intermarriage between them is not common.

As descendants of slaves, Creoles themselves complained about discrimination in a society they felt had always discriminated against them as a people of African heritage.

In fact, the counter-charge of discrimination against the descendants of African slaves has played a major role in fuelling ethnic and group consciousness among the Creoles – and among the Garifunas – even during the best of times when the people who complain seem to be doing relatively well in this multi-racial and multi-cultural society.

There is a perception that ethnic and cultural consciousness in Belize is not as high as it may seem. It's seen as a relatively mild phenomenon because of the harmony that exists among the different groups which collectively constitute the nation of Belize.

But there is also the perception that such consciousness has always existed even if in latent form. And there is also plenty of evidence to show that such consciousness rises sharply in times of crisis when some groups feel threatened by others including new arrivals.

Professor Ralph Premdas of the University of the West Indies has provided another perspective on this phenomenon in the Belizean context in the following terms:

"Is Belize a place where ethnic group consciousness is strong?

Are members of the eight ethnic communities in Belize deeply immersed in their group so that much of individual behaviour can be explained from their membership?

Does their ethnic membership make them rivals or even antagonists to other communities?

As subjectively held constructs, are these Belizean identities malleable and opportunistically worn and discarded depending on the situation?

Is there an overarching Belizean identity that subordinates ethnic membership to a national idea?

Many persons that I spoke to at first declared themselves Belizean. Especially, this was the response from Creole and Garifuna persons in Belize City.

On probing however I did discover the existence of an ethnic map, a consciousness of one's own group identity and an awareness of similar identities among compatriots.

Everyone in Belize that I spoke to had a mental ethnic geography that located him or her comparatively with others. With little prodding, it quickly came out for discussion.

The group that most quickly called itself by its symbolic ethnic marker was the Mayans in Punta Gorda. In fact, at one point I thought that they had arrogated to themselves the sole title of the authentic inhabitants of the country claiming indigenous status.

This however was only a 'mask of confrontation' in relation to their claims for a Maya homeland." – (Ralph R. Premdas, "Belize: Identity and Ethnicity in a Multi-Ethnic State," a paper presented at the Belize Country Conference, University of West Indies, Cave Hill, Barbados, 21 – 24 November 2001).

He goes on to state:

"What is however important in ascribing to oneself an identity is often it subsumes a claim.

Clearly, some of these designations can be dangerous when ascribed collective identities assume the form of hegemonic cultural claims that omit or marginalise the interests and self-definition (of) other communities.

Whether this is done by Mayas in relation to their claims of indigeneity and a homeland or Creoles in relation to their self-ascribed heroic role in founding the Belizean state, it all underscores the point that identities are potentially dangerous constructs in multi-ethnic states. They can be manipulated against other groups for material and symbolic gains, even promoting oppressive ends as Edward Said pointed out.[20]

Many issues in Belize have become ethnicized and racialised.

Writing an article entitled 'Towards An Understanding of Racism in Belize' in the SPEAR newsletter, *IDEAS*, Garifuna Kathrine Mendez argued that the legacy of colonialism and slavery in creating a multi-racial and multi-ethnic society had reverberated in widespread prejudice and discrimination. She said:

'One of the legacies of this system is racism, which we deny exists in Belize. Inter-ethnic and cross-racial hostility also exists in Belize. What we try to do is convince ourselves that we live in peaceful coexistence with each other or that racism is relatively mild in Belize.'[21]

She continues her argument about the impact of the colonial past saying 'those systems continue to be perpetuated today in different forms and with different levels of sophistication.'[22]

She gave several cases in her experience to illustrate her position of which two will be cited.

Case 1: 'A Mestizo teacher in Orange Walk explaining to his Standard IV students that his children are not accustomed to black people and if a black person stayed at his home and woke up in the nite, his children would run.'

Case 2: 'My Mestizo neighbour in Orange Walk whose home I used to visit telling a Mayan man in Spanish not to be afraid of her dog because it would bite only people of colour.'[23]

Ms. Mendez went (on) to describe her own experience with being called by ethnic derogatory epithets pointing to the larger picture of ethnic groups in their own privacy referring to others by uncomplimentary slurs. She said that she was called 'kerub,' 'negrita salmbambu,' 'caribita' etc."
– (Ralph R. Premdas, ibid. See also, cited by Premdas in his essay, Edward Said, "East Isn't East", *Times Literary Supplement*, February, 1995, p. 3; and Kathrine Mendez, "Towards an Understanding of Racism in Belize", *IDEAS* (SPEAR), Vol. 6, No.1, July, 2001, p. 6).

Professor Premdas himself witnessed some of this stereotypical characterisation and racism during his study tour of Belize in April 2001. As he states in his essay:

"While travelling through Belize, I did run into the use of many derogatory ethnic names apart from 'coolie.' They included 'pania' for Mestizos, among others.

Stereotypes are often found as part of the package in ethnic name calling.

None of this is surprising in practically any multi-ethnic society. What is interesting about Belize is the 'hush hush' way it is articulated and practised. It may well be much more insidious than the appearance of open inter-racial cordiality may suggest.

The charge by a major newspaper editor of Belize that society is marked by an ideology of 'colourism' is as disturbing as it is suggestive.

Probably the issue that has drawn most commentary along ethnic and racial lines is migration.

Like a hydra-headed monster, it has assumed many

forms.

In relation to the issue of citizenship and belonging, while it was repeatedly asserted that Belize was 'a country of migrants,' a statement found everywhere in schoolbooks and tourist literature alike, the problem of priority in migration has become contentious.

No ethnic community is prepared to take a back seat to the claims for priority and status by another community, each seeking instead to indiginise itself in its own historiography.

Migration has taken a severe toll on the fate of the 'alien' Central American community. Anthropologist Mark Moberg had described the impact of the entry of cheap Central American workers on the attitude of Belizean workers:

'Conflict between ethnic groups which originated in many instances from displacement of high-paid Belizean workers by immigrants has increasingly assumed a phenotypic, cultural and linguistic dimension.'[24]

The workplace in the production of bananas and citrus is now marked by ethnic stratification and stereotypical rigidities with Creole, Garifuna, and Maya employees likely to be found in supervisory roles while the 'aliens' serve as manual field workers.[25]

But the Central American presence has taken a larger societal toll. While those who seek to defend the migrants underline their contribution to the development of farming expertise and skills in Belize, the rest of the Belizean population and the media lambaste them as unwelcome criminals:

'Given daily recitations in the media of the alleged criminality, violence, and racism of the Central American migrants, it is not surprising that the newcomers have not been well received.'[26]

In a report by the United Nations High Commission for Refugees in Belize, it was observed that 'there are unfortunately numerous stories of refugees who have been objects of racial harassment, assaults by Creole youths, or mistreatment at the hands of the police.'[27]

In public places, the harassment has been described in more detail:

'In public, Belizean youths often relish humiliating jokes at the migrants' expense; in shops central Americans may be pushed aside and told frequently by Belizeans to wait; on buses they lose their seats to Belizean passengers. Entering a bar, frequently migrants may be loudly greeted with 'Go home, Paisa, we do not want aliens here.' *Paisa*, short for *paisano*, alternates in private speech with such overly derogatory references as 'Yellow-bellied Pania' (Spaniards).'[28]

The harassment and assaults in turn have been met by similar racial epithets and stereotypes in which Afro-Belizeans are described as indolent, obstreperous, and primitive." – (Ralph R. Premdas, ibid. See also, cited by Premdas in his paper, Mark Moberg, *Myths of Ethnicity and Nation: Immigration, Work and Identity in the Belize Banana Industry* (Knoxville: University of Tennessee Press, 1997); Mark Moberg, *Citrus, Strategy and Class in Belize* (Iowa: University of Iowa, 1992); Tommie Sue Montgomery, "Refugees in Belize: Belize 1991." *Report of the UNHCR*, Belmopan).

Even though the use of such crude language is not an omnipresent phenomenon, it's disturbing nonetheless and remains a daily occurrence in different parts of the country without always being noticed by the larger society.

Then there is the perennial problem of immigration, even if the country is no longer "inundated" by waves of immigrants from other parts of Central Africa as it was in the 1980s and sometimes even in early 1990s. As Ralph Premdas states:

"The language of insult and counter insult has today gone underground but the underlying attitudes persist making this a sore area of inter-ethnic relations in Belize.

As central Americans adopt Belizean permanent residence and citizenship, relations have moderated with the testimony of several cases of inter-marriages between the Black community and them. The stigma persist nevertheless kept alive by the continued entry of Central Americans into Belize albeit at a lesser pace than the 1980s.

Migration has also become a perennial issue in the general elections of the country with ethnic overtones entangled. This is indisputably a sensitive site where the ethnic factor has periodically merged with political campaign rhetoric as a strongly articulated force.

Specifically, the influx of 'aliens' from Central America and the fears that it has triggered has been capitalised upon by the United Democratic Party against the People's United Party which has been accused as sympathetic to Guatemala.

While both parties are multi-ethnic, it is generally perceived that the UDP has a hard core of Creole support and the PUP a similar level of Mestizo adherents.

Generally, however, the two parties are not ethnically based formations and they have each taken power winning and losing the same constituencies in different elections.

In the 1984 elections, the UDP openly charged the PUP regime with encouraging Central American migration as a method to 'Latinise' the electorate. Anthropologist Nigel Bolland articulated these points:

'In fact one of the most important consequences of Guatemala's persistent claim to Belize has been the perception of internal disunity and mutual suspicions with Creoles in particular fearing recolonisation.

The Guatemalan threat encourages Creole Belizeans to continue to think of the Spanish-speaking Maya and Mestizo Belizean as the British thought of them, namely as representatives of an alien culture.

Many Creoles feel that Belize is and should remain a predominantly English-speaking country and fear that the 'latinization' of Belize will displace them.'[29]

The PUP was defeated and again in the 1993 elections with the same result. Even today, some still make the same argument alleging that the PUP had registered the 'aliens' for political gain.

There is the stigma that has stuck that the PUP is pro-'aliens' and pro-Central American with the subterranean subtext that it is also a Mestizo-dominated party that has defined Belizean identity not as Caribbean but Central American.

There is an ethnic shadow involved in these associations. Echoes of this perceived ethnic polarisation at election time is now heard in the view that Dean Barrow as a Creole leader of the UDP will not be elected as Prime Minister in the next elections.

The two occasions when the UDP wrested power from the PUP occurred when its leader, Manuel Esquivel, was a Mestizo.

The larger point however suggests that there is for political purposes an alliance between the Creole and Garifuna community versus the Hispanics and Mayas. This is yet to be proven decisively but there are suggestive intimations outlining this ominous (trend).

The instigator of this alignment of ethnic forces into the political partisan realm would clearly be assigned in part to the two migratory processes of Central American influx and Creole-Garifuan outflow resulting in Mestizo ascendancy." – (Ralph R. Premdas, ibid. See also, cited by Premdas in his essay, Nigel Bolland, "Ethnicity, Pluralism, and Politics in Belize", in *Identity, Ethnicity, and Culture in the Caribbean* edited by Ralph R. Premdas (Trinidad: School of Continuing Studies, University of the West Indies, 2000), p. 11).

When Professor Premdas wrote that in 2001, Dean Barrow was the leader of the opposition party. The People's United Party (PUP) was then still in power.

And the sentiment expressed by some Belizeans that he would not be elected prime minister of Belize in the next elections was a reflection of the political climate in the country during that time. But he proved them wrong when he later won and became the country's first black prime minister in 2008. It was an important milestone in the history of the country.

But that does not mean ethnic rivalries don't exist in the political arena which has accommodated players from all ethno-cultural groups with varying degrees of success through the years.

What it demonstrates is that when there are issues which affect all groups, and when different groups share interests in a number of areas, the people can transcend ethnic loyalties and pursue common goals united by a common agenda.

The people of Belize have also succeeded in covering up ethnic rivalries and tensions, which continue to bubble under the surface, in a way many people in other countries have not been able to.

But that does not solve the problem; nor does it mean that all Belizeans share the perception that their country is an island of tranquility in a sea of turmoil in the Central American region; although it is comparatively.

There are many who are vocal and make it clear that racism and ethnic rivalries and even hostilities are a problem in Belize even if it's not a major one as it is in some countries. And as Ralph Premdas states:

"Overall, it is safe to infer from the materials that I have been exposed to that ethnic consciousness is pervasive evoked in some situations more than others.

The raw materials of ethnic consciousness are visible

but not dense and overwhelming so as to define every situation or crisis.

Ethnic identity in Belize, embedded in aspects of language, religious and regional differences, is not a badge that appears to be always worn so that it dominates every action and inspires every plan.

In some ethnically inflamed societies such as Guyana and Northern Ireland, and Sri Lanka, ethnic symbols as an emblem of identity are inscribed in practically all spheres of life and in individual choices. This is not the case in Belize.

In negotiating life's daily challenges, other parameters assume salience such as economic interests.

Most Belizeans seem to operate on the basis that socio-economic standing determines life chances more so than membership in an ethnic community.

They are found in many inter-ethnic associations and workplaces together sharing space and camaraderie. Families expend monies to improve their children's educational preparation so that they may acquire decent jobs.

While certain groups may feel disadvantaged because of historical background or cultural practices such as the Mayas, there appears to be a sentiment that education and training can overcome these barriers towards individual betterment.

All of this is not to gainsay the argument that there is a greater incidence of poverty among some ethnic groups than others. What it argues is that there is no overt system of closure that creates rigid ethno-economic compartments like a caste order. There is more classism than ethnicism at some levels of life in Belize.

There may be silent prejudices against those who are not Black or Central American, but there is upward mobility everywhere and large concentrations of middle class Blacks as well as large concentrations of Poor Whites. In effect, there is little consistent correlative coincidence between colour and economic wellbeing in Belize.

Do ethnicity and colour matter in Belize then? In some ways for some persons suggesting structural bottlenecks in mobility for some but not a universal practice that pigeonholes people into rigid stratified ethno-economic compartments.

In a society that is multi-ethnic and derived from a colonial system that espoused a hierarchy of races and ethnicities, it would take time for all the accretions of the past in terms of prejudice and racism to be completely jettisoned.

However, it is quite conceivable that in place of colour and ethnicity especially among the well off, a new order of hierarchy can emerge based on clientelistic practices having very little to do with race and ethnic category.

New forms of colour blind oppressions can emerge out of clientelistic, family and clan networks cutting across ethnicity and race. Some of this is already evident in Belize." – (Ralph R. Premdas, Ibid.).

Although there are people in Belize who have transcended ethnicity and ethno-cultural loyalties, there is also a reawakening among some Belizeans in terms of cultural revival and pride in their ancestral roots. One very good example of this is the increasing interest in Africa among Belizeans of African ancestry.

There is also very strong interest in Maya culture and history among the Maya, a consciousness that sometimes borders on racism against black Belizeans who have always been stigmatised as an inferior people because of their origin and history as descendants of African slaves.

Groups of relatively new immigrants such as the Chinese and East Indians also have shown a degree of ethnic and cultural consciousness that's manifested in a number of ways including pride in their heritage and ancestral homelands even if some of them don't know much about China and India just as many black Belizeans who show great pride in Africa know very little about their African motherland.

It is a consciousness that will probably always exist in Belize because, as a multicultural society, the people are expected and expect to cherish their identities not as members of a society which wants to dilute or abolish those identities and their cultures but one that respects them on the basis of unity in diversity.

In fact, there is evidence everywhere showing that the different racial and ethno-cultural groups in Belize are determined to preserve their identities and promote their cultures. As Professor Irma McClaurin states in her book *Women of Belize: Gender and Change in Central America*:

"In different communities throughout Belize, efforts at cultural preservation are occurring – not just among the Garifuna, who have established their own cultural council and hold an annual conference on Garinagu life and culture, but also among the Maya, who attempt to transmit to their children the music, dances, foods, and lifeways that make them culturally unique.

Increasingly, Creoles have joined in to preserve their own distinctive culture, especially with regard to language, food, and music.

The central aim of all these ventures is to document the elements that embody Belize's cultural heritage." – (Irma McClaurin, *Women of Belize: Gender and Change in Central America*, Newark, New Jersey: Rutgers University Press, 1 August 1996, p. 34).

There are different perspectives on this subject, some different from mine. And there are those which are not much different from what I have stated in this book. Professor Ralph Premdas is one of the people who have addressed the subject of ethno-cultural consciousness in Belize and has reached his own conclusion after answering

75

a question he has raised here:

"How much ethno-cultural consciousness exists in Belize? Is there a cultural revival in progess today?

Anthropologist Dr. Joseph Palacio has observed that with the improvement of economic conditions in Belize, there is a cultural revival in part aimed at procuring access to opportunities and resources. Said Palacio:

'The prevailing spirit of tolerance, the opening up of roads, the availability of wage labour and improved facilities for education and health together created opportunities for ethnic groups to re-evaluate their status as Belizeans. Among the Maya, Garifuna, and Mestizo, there has been a process of ethnic revivalism and even ethnogenesis.'[31]

By ethnogenesis, I assume that he means the attempt by each community to write its own experiential narratives and record its historical memory.

History is often deployed as a tool of re-constructing a community's image of itself especially if it had been colonised or placed in a position of subordination and exploitation. Its narratives define the image of the group and asserts its demand for dignity and recognition.

Mythmaking is important to identity formation, and in Belize, intellectual leaders of the ethno-cultural associations construct their own version of historical reality with a view to promoting not only their symbolic representation but to advance their claims for material resources.

There is a veritable historiographical war in progress as witnessed just recently by an editorial headline in the *Amandala* newspaper entitled: "The Battle of Belize".[32]

The editorial discussed versions of Belizean history which are being promulgated by different groups. Apart from these symbolic roles, it also serves instrumental claims as Palacio underscores in the Belizean ethno-cultural revival underway:

'Particularly in the case of Belize, the Garifuna and Maya are using ethnicity as a method of inserting themselves into the new Belizean nation thereby being able to extract socio-economic benefits for themselves and their progeny.'[33]" – (Ralph R. Premdas, ibid. See also, cited by Premdas in his essay, Joseph M. Palacio, "May the New Creole of Belize Please Rise", *IDEAS* (Spear), Vol. 6, No. 1, August 2001, p. 3; and "The Battle of Belize," *Amandala*, 12 August, 2002, p. 10).

Even groups which have completely lost their original cultures from their ancestral homelands show a remarkable degree of cultural pride and ethnic consciousness. Descendants of immigrants from India are a typical example of that in Belize.

Black Belizeans are not very much different in that context. They also lost their African cultures and ethnic identities through slavery. Yet many of them show great pride in their African ancestry and cultural heritage as much as East Indians in Belize do.

Professor Ralph Premdas himself is a descendant of those Indians although they settled in another country, British Guiana, now Guyana, where they were taken by the British colonial rulers to work as indentured servants and on sugar plantations.

And he is proud of his identity as a descendant of coolies even though the term is often used as an insult. It has derogatory connotations which have nothing to do with its original meaning.

Cultural revival and consciousness has become a national phenomenon in Belize even if it's not strongly expressed in all cases. But there are people in every ethnic group who take the matter very seriously. As Professor Premdas states in his paper, "Belize: Identity and Ethnicity in a Multi-Ethnic State":

"The group that was most curious in terms of attachment to an ethnic community was the East Indians.

Having lost practically all their old values in religion and rituals including the loss of traditional Indian names, food, and attire, they still seemed to think that they were Indians but only in a secondary sense of belonging to Belize first.

One young Indian from Corozal told me that when his secondary school put up a program to highlight Belize's ethnic diversity, he was chosen to exemplify East Indians but that he knew practically nothing about them and wanted to know about 'his culture.'

The East Indian Cultural Council has made it as part of its program to learn more about Indians in the Caribbean and to recover something of their lost Indiannness.

In a sort of cultural revival that is currently going on in Belize, they will literally have to invent their Indianness.

When I met the representative of the Kreyol (Creole) Cultural Council in Punta Gorda, they took me into her little museum of Creole artefacts indicating to me that this was an important project that was necessary for the survival of Creole memory.

Similarly, Garifuna leaders such as Roy Caeytano had lamented the increasing loss of their language and way of life and were keen about reviving it.

The Garifuna with whom I had contact articulated and affirmed a Garifuna identity not necessarily superimposed on their Belizean identity but parallel to it.

While it would be an exaggeration to say that there was an ethno-cultural war going on at low key in Belize, it was clear that the different ethnic communities had come to realise that unless they get organised and mobilised as in their respective cultural associations, they would get little of the rights, resources, and power to which they feel entitled.

The struggle over the land claims of the Maya and over

the control of the Toledo Development Corporation illustrate the mobilisation of ethnic identities for protection and profit.

I had expected to discover a full-blown ethnic struggle between Creoles and Mestizos over the demographical change of their relative numbers especially protestations from Creoles over their dramatically diminished standing. What I found instead was a symbolic one-way war in which the Creole group continues to celebrate in the mythology of the battle of St. George's Quay their priority over others (sic).

In response, there is a remarkable quiet among Mestizos about their identity or numbers to the point of being defensive. In fact, I could not find an exclusive Mestizo Cultural Association but instead a tiny regional Maya-Mestizo Cultural Council which has little to do with the main body of Mestizos. It seemed that they were the least overtly organised as a cultural community.

The Mestizos however were very strongly represented in politics and commerce and a number of prominent Mestizo names crop up among the wealthiest families in Belize.

They do resent being misidentified as Maya or Central American, and as one educated Mestizo woman told me, they go about in their daily existence denying their part-Maya identity.

They are very quietly educating their children in the best schools in Belize and, as one Creole newspaper editor remarked, they do not like the Creoles go into classical subjects but into commerce and science. I was told that St. John's College, the finest secondary school in Belize, is where they all go.

It is clear that the Mestizos are very much conscious of themselves as a community specifically descended from the Yucatan in the mid-1980s and have as much right as anyone else to be called 'indigenous' to the land and in building Belize.

Mestizos are mindful that they have overcome the demographical pre-eminence of the Creoles but seem unwilling to flout this fact into an assertive claim for rights or resources.

They are however slowly 'encroaching' on the public bureaucracy which has been dominated for so long by Creoles so that as one person remarked to me 'they are now found everywhere in the civil service.'

Clearly, there was an unevenness in attachment to their groups, with some wearing their ethnic sub-national identity very lightly while others very strongly.

There were some forces and factors that appeared as unifying towards establishing a commonly shared Belizeanness which Andy Palacio described well as Punta Rock, fear of Guatemala, rice, beans and stew chicken, and the English language.

I suspect that there are some issues which tend to arouse ethnic assertions and others which do not.

On the question of Creole supercession by Mestizos, I gather that Creoles as Creoles are galvanised around their loss of status and power.

Generally, ethnic labels are not overtly exhibited and not turned into a symbol of collective mobilisation suggesting that other factors are at work qualifying the role of ethnicity in daily life such as crime, drugs, unemployment, HIV-AIDS, corruption, etc.

Is there a hierarchy of ethnic groups? What is the structural nature of the mosaic? Are ethnic boundaries being erased and a melting pot being fashioned?

With self-determination in self-government and the departure of the British, Belizeans were put in charge of their own homeland. Already, many old hierarchies built around European dominance were modified and old economic structures that maintained disparities were removed. A new economy was being fashioned with private business and the public service offering employment and income.

While in the past the public service had become the carrier of status and respect, in the contemporary period it faced challenges from new industries and economic endeavours.

Skills and training were becoming the definers of economic wellbeing for most of the population. A good deal of this was determined by non-ethnic criteria.

There is extensive inter-racial mixing in Belize creating a population that is increasingly becoming 'brown.'

It is easy to imagine that there is a melting pot in the making in the creation of a new Belizean person. This sort of optimism must be tempered by the Caribbean experience where new forms of racism and ethnic formations have evolved in the context of new mixes.

One needs to remember that ethnic groups as self-conscious collective communities are created from fictive diacritica. Colour and race are only one set of data that entire the construction of the ethnic mix (sic).

Region, religion, values, language, etc can contribute to a differentiation of people of the same colour or race into separate ethnic formations.

The racial mixing therefore cannot mean more tolerance and less racism.

Is there an overarching Belizeanness and a Belizean nationalism? If it exists, it has little to do with racial mixing and more to do with shared experiences in sacrifice and suffering.

The Guatemalan border and its inherent fears offer a shared dimension of life. So does the English language and extensive bilingualism. Some food such as rice and beans and stew chicken as well as some musical forms like Punta Rock offer uniting strands.

Against the unifying factors are many disuniting ones such as poverty and inequality which divide citizens.

The political system seems to be a commonly shared arena of collective debate and decision making but it is suspect by too many citizens. While election turnout has been very high by any standards, it does not point to a sense of citizen efficacy and participation.

Race and ethnicity have not asserted themselves in the political process so that political mobilisation is cleaved around these factors. This is a good thing in so far as it points to a fluid situation in which citizen partisan loyalty cannot be taken for granted.

Political discourse however seems to be very strident. Radio talk shows have emerged along with a proliferation of civil society groups pointing to a measure of citizen engagement in influencing governmental decision-making."

Belize is a mosaic. It is a tapestry whose various strands have been intricately woven to create one of the most tantalizing pieces of the human fabric.

At the core of its success is its ability to avoid ethnic conflicts which have wreaked havoc in other societies in spite of the fact that ethnic tensions do exist in Belize and will probably continue to be a way of life in a society that has not achieved full integration.

It is not a melting pot but one of the best examples of unity in diversity. There is a national consciousness and it supersedes ethnic loyalties even though the existence of these ethno-cultural entities is an integral part of Belize's national identity and life.

Part Two:

The People of Belize

BELIZE is a heterogeneous society. It's the most ethnically and racially diverse country in Central America. It's also one of the most diverse – racially, culturally, and ethnically – in Latin America and in the Caribbean.

All this diversity is rooted in history. The country is a product of history more than anything else. Even its demographic configuration, coinciding with regional identity partly shaped by geography, is a product of history.

One of the major events which have shaped the nation's destiny is slavery. Even the nation's demographic composition was largely determined by this abominable institution for centuries.

As far back as 1750, about 75 per cent of the people in the British settlement were slaves. At least 10 per cent were whites. The rest were free blacks. The indigenous people were not counted in the 1750 census.

Belize society today is ethnically diverse and culturally rich as never before. Historically it's a country of immigrants. Even most of the indigenous people – the Maya – have ancestral ties to Mexico or Guatemala.

The ancestors of the Mestizo, a product of indigenous and Spanish intermarriages and other relationships, migrated from the Yucatán in southeastern Mexico.

Two groups have African roots in addition to other ancestries. These are the Kriols and the Garifuna.

During most of the 1900s, Creoles were the largest ethnic group in British Honduras – later Belize – followed by Mestizos, Garifunas, and the Maya.

But there have been major demographic changes through the years. According to the 1991 census, Mestizos outnumbered Creoles.

This multi-ethnic country is also home to communities of German Mennonites, Chinese, East Indians, and immigrants from the Middle East.

Ethnic and geographic identification coincides with the areas where ethnic groups settled.

In the northern and western parts of the country, the Mestizo are the dominant group.

In the central part of Belize are Kriols or Creoles. Many of them are a product of interracial relationships between African slaves as well as their descendants and the British settlers. They have also intermarried with other people.

In the south are the Garifuna and the Maya. The Garifuna live mainly along the coast. The Maya live mostly in the interior.

The Garifuna, also known as Black Caribs, have indigenous roots traced to the Caribbean islands. But they are easily identified by their African ancestry more than anything else.

One of the major factors in Belize's demographic configuration has been immigration.

Although the country has an indigenous population, Belize is essentially a land of immigrants who have migrated there since colonial times.

The country's demographic profile has changed even in recent years, especially with the influx of Spanish-speaking immigrants from neighbouring countries who sought refuge and sanctuary in Belize in the 1980s because of civil strife in their home countries.

This demographic shift and reconfiguration of Belize has fuelled ethnic consciousness especially among those who consider themselves to be truly Belizean. It's the fear of being swamped by foreigners. They also feel that they're being marginalised.

The group that embodies these sentiments probably more than any other is the Creole, especially those who identify themselves as black. As Professor Anne Sutherland states in her book *The Making of Belize: Globalization in The Margins*:

"Another factor influencing the increase in ethnic identity issues is the change in demographics in Belize since the late 1980s.

A real demographic shift showed up in the 1990 census, with Afro-Belizeans dropping from 48 to 36 percent of the population, while the mestizo population increased from 33 to 44 percent (Woods, Perry, and Steagall 1995).

An article in *The Houston Chronicle*, 'Belize Finds Melting Pot may Be Coming to a Boil – Creole Population Faces Uneasy Changes' (Gunson, 1996), highlights the Creoles' fears about what they call the 'latinization' of Belize and the increasing emigration of Creoles to the United States in large numbers.

Recent calls for Creoles to link with their 'Garifuna African brothers' is a response to these changes." – (Anne Sutherland, *The Making of Belize: Globalization in The Margins*, New York: Bergin & Garvey, 30 July 1998, p. 84).

Common interest, as well as self-interest, is the

primary motivation in the quest for this kind of solidarity. Yet there are some Garifunas who feel that Creoles who advocate unity between the two groups in pursuit of a common cause are motivated by self-interest – Creole interest and the well-being of the Creole community – more than anything else. For, why would a people who considered them to be socially inferior want to unite with them? It's a matter of political expediency.

However in the context of Belize, faced by "a common enemy" who wants to marginalise Africans or people of African descent, such insults – which some may contend were in the past – may be overlooked.

It's all about power. As Sutherland states:

"With a small national population, the slightest change in demographics has an important impact on the political balance between ethnic groups.

During the 1980s, when civil wars in El Salvador and Guatemala, and political unrest in Nicaragua and Honduras, were at their peak, the flow of Central American refugees into Belize gave the country one of the highest rates of immigration relative to current population of any country in the world (Ropp 1995).

More important, the relative position of the the two largest ethnic groups, Spanish (mestizo) and Creole, shifted.

With the mestizo population now larger than the Creole nationwide (although Belize district and most civil service jobs are still predominantly occupied by Creoles), the political ties to Central America are stronger than ever and the issues that most concern the Spanish-speaking population must be addressed politically.

These include the teaching of Spanish in the schools and a strong reaction against the push by Creoles, who want Creole taught in the schools (Gillett 1996).

Although Belize has been a member of CARICOM for some time, it did not join the OAS until August 15, 1995, a move that has been linked directly to establishing closer strategic ties with Central America (World Wide Web, Belize Information Service).

A local television program titled 'The Mestization of Belize,' made by Great Belize Productions, illustrates the ethnic tension. In this documentary, the editor of *Amandala*, a newspaper that explicitly promotes black pride and consciousness, calls mestization 'a problem' that will result in Belize losing its 'character." – (Ibid., pp. 84 – 85).

The question that arises is this: In a mutli-racial and multi-ethnic society like Belize, which group defines the nation's character?

And who has the right to say you are a true Belizean or you are not – simply because you don't belong to the group of those who try to define you?

The most vocal group is, of course, black. And the people from this group who articulate the position that they are true Belizeans, while Mestizos are not, have been accused of racism:

"When questioned about this 'racist' point of view, he (the editor of *Amandala*) responds that if promoting his race is racism, then he has to live with that label, but he wants the government to 'do something' about keeping blacks in Belize in order to counter the immigration of Central Americans.

In the same program, other Creoles disagree. A representative from SPEAR argues that since this shift was inevitable, the government should have seen it coming and should have prepared people for the psychological change.

The late Topsy Harriat, director of the Department of Archaeology in Belize at the time, and also a Creole, pointed out that this had happened before, during the Caste Wars, when some 7,000 mestizos became Belizeans, overwhelming the 3,000 Creoles; but Belize still kept its character.

The program illustrates the threat that recent migrations pose for the previously predominant Belize district Creoles." – (Ibid., p. 85).

It also demonstrates the complexity of life in a multi-racial and multi-ethnic society and how national unity can be severely tested when people of different races, cultures and ethnic backgrounds do not necessarily believe that they are one people who belong to the same nation and who should transcend ethnic loyalties for the sake of national unity.

In fact, some Belizeans concede that has indeed been the case. And it probably still is the case today, although it is hard to give a specific number of how many Belizeans feel that way. But, as Dr. Angel E. Cal, president of the University of Belize, states:

"It was not until the advent of a national road grid in the 1960s and the birth of the nationalist movement in the 1950s that some Belizeans started to think in terms of Belize as a political concept....

Indigenous people in the Americas have long suffered from the violence meted out by both the institutionalized power of the state and the deep-rooted racism that continues to characterize the very unequal terms in which indigenous people relate with other groups in society....

The Maya are the people who have the least voice and the least power of any sort and continue to have the least access to basic social amenities, including elementary education, basic health care, and suitable housing.

The Maya are the people who can least access land, credit, and other public supported services taken for ranted by other sectors of the population.

Why did this happen, why does it continue to happen and, more importantly, what can be done to break the continuous cycle of poverty that has been the hallmark of the poorest of the poor of Mesoamerica?....

The British conveniently categorized both the indigenous Belizean Maya and the Mayan immigrants of the 1800s as 'aliens.' This categorization justified treating the Maya en bloc as outsiders of what they regarded as their colony of Belize.

Mayan existence was practically denied by the British authorities. They were rendered invisible. For example, prior to the census of 1861, no attempt was made to count the indigenous Maya. The 1861 census lumped all the Maya as immigrants.

Today, we find that the myth is being used for a more sinister purpose. There is the palpable tendency to treat the Maya as 'aliens' and to therefore dismiss Mayan claims for fair treatment as a community. It is used to justify the attitude towards the Maya as late-coming 'aliens' who have no right to claim any special consideration as a community.

The myth also subtly rationalizes in the minds of many Belizeans the racism that the Maya continue to suffer in the land of their ancestors....

Th(e) perception persists today that the Maya are just one among the several immigrant groups that came to live in Belize and as such they cannot advance any special claim on the land of their ancestors." – " – (Angel E. Cal, "Racism Against the Maya in Belize," paper presented to Select Faculty from the University of Louisville, Kentucky, USA, 25th February, 2000).

The complex nature of ethnic identity in Belize, compounded by racism against some groups, is a product of historical dictates and contemporary realities which have intermingled and intersected to create one of the most fascinating societies in modern history.

Each group has its own perspective on reality. And each group pursues its own interests, not necessarily to the detriment of national unity, but for its own wellbeing as they all continue to navigate the complex terrain that is Belize; a nation that is a product of many peoples and cultures and which continues to be an experiment in true integration amidst ethnic tensions.

Only Belizeans can resolve the contradictions within. And only they can best define ethnicity in their own context. It's a complex phenomenon; a point underscored by Anne Sutherland when she states:

"Ethnic issues in Belize are highly complex and multicultural.

There is a push for greater identity with Africa by a small but vocal intelligentsia; there is a national demographic shift from a predominance of Creoles to a predominance of mestizos; there are contested language issues; and the Garifuna are enjoying a revival in cultural pride after a long history of cultural repression.

In addition, the Maya are entangled in a conflict with ethnic dimensions.

An interesting development is the appearance of an umbrella organization – the Belize National Ethnic Organization (BENIC) – for ethnic groups that includes the Garifuna Cultural Council, the Toledo Cultural Council, and the Alacalde Cultural Council, the last both Maya organizations.

BENIC represents 18 percent of the population of Belize. The Maya consciousness movement is illustrative of the way that ethnicity, cloaked in primordial language, comes to turn on more concrete issues concerned with historical structures of inequality." – (Ibid.).

Although immigration has played a major role in shaping the nation's identity and the identities of different ethno-cultural groups in the country, other forces also, in varying degrees, have shaped Belize's demographic landscape and composition in its history. The main ones from a historical point of view were colonisation and slavery.

Because of all those forces, Belize has evolved into a country of unique characteristics. It's a country of many cultures, languages, ethnic groups and identities which have been shaped without parallel in the region of Central America, if not in the entire Latin America.

Its demographic composition alone is a subject of an interesting study without even looking at the multiple identities – cultural and ethnic – which collectively constitute the nation of Belize.

Out of the country's more than 320,000 people according to 2010 statistics, Mestizos constitute 34 per cent of the total population; Kriols 25 per cent; Spanish 15 per cent; Maya 11 per cent; and Garifuna 6 per cent.

The Maya, or Mayans, are the oldest inhabitants of the region that came to be known as Belize. They have lived in what is now Belize and the Yucatán region since the second millennium B.C.

But the majority of Belize's original Maya population was wiped out by disease and conflicts between the indigenous tribes and the British settlers.

Today, there are three Maya groups in Belize.

There are the Yucatec who fled from Yucatán, Mexico, during the Caste War of the 1840s.

There are the Mopan who are indigenous to Belize but who were subjugated and expelled by the British settlers. They fled to Guatemala. They returned to Belize in the 1800s to escape from enslavement by the Spanish settlers in Guatemala.

And there are the Kekchi who also fled from slavery in Guatemala during the same period.

The Mopan and the Kekchi live mostly in Toledo District. They constitute the largest percentage of the descendants of the Maya in Belize today. And they have remained the most traditional and most culturally distinct among all the people of Belize. But their original homeland is Guatemala.

Of the three Maya groups, only the Mopan can claim indigenous status on the land that became Belize. Yet they're among the most disadvantaged in their ancestral homeland. Their ancestral roots are in the western part of Belize and across the border in the Peten region of Guatemala.

The Mopan lost their land when the British settlers moved farther west in their quest for territorial expansion and in pursuit of their business interests in the lumber industry. The settlers came into conflict with the indigenous Mopan whom they forced to flee to Guatemala. Many of them also perished from disease.

But they returned to Belize from Guatemala. The modern Mopan arrived in the southern part of what was then British Honduras in 1886. They settled in the area that is now Toledo District and founded the town of San Antonio.

The town is a Maya stronghold and one of the main centres of indigenous culture in Belize.

San Antonio also is the largest Mopan settlement in the country.

Mopan society today is not much different from what it used to be hundreds of years ago. Little has changed. Most of the people live as simple peasants. And they have strong family units which collectively constitute a network of support in their communities similar to extended families in Africa.

Their main food crops are beans, maize, rice, tubers, cacao and sugar cane. They also grow cash crops including citrus fruits. But because of poverty, most of them have not been able to make a transition from subsistence farming to modern agriculture.

The other indigenous group, the Kekchi, probably have had the most tragic history of any Mayan group. Their traditional homeland is in Guatemala where they lived as a culturally distinct group. And their language is different from the Mopan language.

But the indigenous groups share a common identity as Maya in spite of the ethnic and cultural diversity among them. There are no Maya or Mayans as a single ethnic and cultural group. There are, instead, many ethnic and cultural groups which collectively constitute the Maya.

The history of the Kekchi in Belize starts from the 1870's and 1880's when large numbers of them escaped from Guatemala.

The Mestizos in Guatemala, together with the Spanish rulers, mobilised forces against the indigenous people in order to take seize their land and institute severe economic reforms which would deprive the native people of their rights and turn them into slaves in their own homeland, working for their Spanish conquerors.

The Kekchi were among the biggest victims. They lost their land. Attempts were also made to force the indigenous people to work for white farmers as slaves, thus forcing them to flee their homeland.

Like the Mopan, they also settled in Toledo District in southern Belize and established the community of San Pedro de Colombia. But they also settled in other parts of the district.

Their forced migration to British Honduras – not long before it became a colony in 1862 – also resulted in the loss of some of their ethnic and cultural identity because of intermingling with other people.

Through the years, the Kekchi have mixed with some Mopan groups and have therefore not fully retained their ethnic and cultural identity although it remains largely intact.

The Kekchi are also the poorest people in Belize. But they're known for their communal lifestyle. They have also played a major role in the revival and preservation of the Mayan heritage through the years.

Whites are another major group in Belize as they have been for more than 300 years since the country was founded in the 1600s.

Initially, Spanish conquistadors explored the region that's now known as Belize and declared the land a Spanish colony. But they decided not to settle there because the area did not have natural resources such as gold. But they still claimed the region as part of Spain because it was surrounded by territories which had been seized by the Spanish settlers.

Later, English and Scottish settlers and pirates known as Baymen entered the area in the 16th and 17th centuries respectively and established a settlement which constituted the nucleus of what came to be the colony of British Honduras, and now Belize, as we learned earlier.

All these groups – the indigenous people, the British settlers, African slaves and their descendants as well as immigrants from other parts of Central America and beyond – have collectively formed one nation in this "tropical paradise" in Central America which has become one of the best and most interesting experiments in multiculturalism.

Many people describe Belize as a "melting pot." But it's not quite that, if at all.

Cultural fusion has taken place in some cases. But Belize is not culturally homogeneous. Its people don't constitute a monolithic whole. It's a land of distinct racial and ethno-cultural entities, each asserting its own identity, while at the same time acknowledging the primacy of national identity as an immutable fact.

Even with the racial intermingling that has taken place through the centuries, racial and ethnic distinctions have not been obliterated.

Major groups such as the Kriol (Creole), Mestizo, Maya, and Garifuna, clearly stand out on the landscape. But smaller groups – East Indians, Chinese and Mennonites – are equally distinct despite their status as minorities.

And there are other groups such as Arabs who, although smaller, have played an important role in the history of Belize. For example, one of the prime ministers of Belize, Said Musa, was half-Arab, tracing his Arab roots to Palestine.

His father immigrated to Belize where Said Musa was born on 19 March 1944. Although his first and last names point to his Arab origin, his middle name, Wilbert, does not.

He served as prime minister from 28 August 1998 to 8 February 2008.

Many other Belizeans of Arab origin have also served at high levels of government. According to a report by Nathan Guttman, "From El Bireh to Belize," in *Haaretz*, a Jewish daily newspaper published in Dallas, Texas, USA:

"The father of the prime minister of Belize was born in El Bireh, while the father of Belize's ambassador to London, and the grandfather of the country's ambassador to Washington, was born in Beit Hanina.

We're not talking about a Palestinian government-in-exile. These are some of the highest-ranking officials in the government of Belize, a 9,000 square-mile Central American country with only two paved roads and a tiny population of 200,000 (60 percent are Catholic).

Though they are but a small demographic presence in the Caribbean country, members of the Palestinian diaspora have secured dominant positions in its parliamentary democracy.

Belize's Arab population numbers a little bit more than 10,000 immigrants. Only six families in this Arab cluster are Palestinian. Yet these Palestinians have become well-entrenched in their new home, joining the political elite.

The father of Belize Prime Minister Said Musa, Hamid Musa, left his home in El Bireh, near Ramallah, in 1930. Economic hardship caused him to wander around the world, looking for a place to start a new life.

Equipped with a British Mandatory passport, Hamid Musa made it to Central America, and put down roots in another colony attached to the British empire: British Honduras, which was to become Belize.

For emigrants from the British Empire in this pre-war period, the Caribbean colony was relatively attractive. Its economy, based on sugar cane cultivation and mahogany export, was stable, and provided a measure of opportunity to workers of various socio-ethnic backgrounds.

In Belize's ethnic landscape, an immigrant from the Middle East could find a niche, alongside descendants of the Mayans, immigrants from various South American countries, and subjects of the British Empire.

Hamid Musa settled in the country, married a native-born woman, and established himself. The couple had eight children. While he continued to speak Arabic with Arab friends, Palestinian and Lebanese immigrants, his children grew up in a new, different culture.

'Unfortunately, in my home we didn't speak Arabic; it was a mixed culture,' Prime Minister Said Musa recalled in a telephone interview. 'My mother played a dominant role in our educational upbringing, and we grew up as part and parcel of Belize's culture.'

Musa says that only one aspect of Arab culture remains as an important part of his childhood memories: He loved Arab food – tehina, kubbe and labaneh.

Journey into the past

As a student in Britain in 1964, Said Musa decided to search for his roots. Together with a Belize friend of Palestinian descent and a few English friends, he set out on a trip to the Middle East. After several long days of hitchhiking in the region, they arrived in Israel; they headed for the West Bank.

'For me, it was an amazing experience,' he recalls. 'I saw where my father came from. I was given a royal welcome in El Bireh – they even slaughtered a sheep in my honor.'

After Israel took control over the West Bank in 1967, Musa remained in touch for a while with relatives he had discovered during this emotional, eye-opening journey. Yet, at some point in the 1970s, the connection faded.

Musa, today 57, returned as a qualified lawyer to Belize after completing studies abroad. He began to work in Belize's government service. Two years later, he joined forces with two other lawyers, and set up a private firm.

One of his law partners, Assad Shoman, also hails from Belize's small Palestinian diaspora community.

Shoman's and Musa's families were very close and thus could be considered virtual Palestinian landsleit: The distance between El Bireh and Beit Hanina, where Shoman's father was born, is not so great.

As working partners, Musa and Shoman did not handle only legal matters. In fact, their office became a hotbed of political activity: The two established the Popular Action Council (PAC).

As time passed, Shoman continued to work as a lawyer, but Musa left law to take up politics full time. He joined the PUP (Popular Union Party), becoming a senator in Belize's parliament in 1974. During his career, he has served as the country's attorney general, education minister and economic development minister.

Musa was one of the writers of Belize's Declaration of Independence. After Belize gained independence from Britain in 1981, he was appointed foreign minister.

Three years ago (in 1998), he led the PUP to victory in national elections, and became prime minister.

Meanwhile, Assad Shoman remained a close friend. After Musa became prime minister, he appointed Shoman ambassador to Britain.

Since Belize remains a member of the British Commonwealth, Shoman's position is formally designated 'High Commissioner in the United Kingdom,' the premier post in Belize's small diplomatic corps.

How have six Palestinian families risen in Belize, and

secured top posts in the small Caribbean country?

Prime Minister Musa denies that the ethnic background is a political factor. 'Nobody voted for me on account of my origins,' he says. 'People voted for me because of what I am and what I stand for. In any event, the Arab community here is so small that [my] ethnic origins can't have any electoral impact.'

Tourism potential

Perched on the sea, Belize is a crossing point between the Caribbean and Central America. It borders Mexico in the north, and Guatemala in the south and west.

Relations with Guatemala are often tense, as Guatemala has territorial claims that stretch into Belize's borders.

Belize's population is diverse: a combination of native Mayans whose roots stretch back thousands of years, descendants of African slaves brought to the area in the 18th century, and offspring of immigrants (both from the British colonial period and also more recent years).

Many immigrants arrived as indigent refugees from Africa, the Middle East and Asia. The country's official language is English, but citizens also speak Creole, Spanish, Maya and Garifuna.

A British colony through the beginning of the 1980s, Belize was one of the last countries in Central America to gain independence.

Its parliamentary democracy today is fashioned after the British model, on a smaller scale (the elected house of representatives has 29 members, and the senate has eight).

The prime minister has executive authority, while the Queen of England is the symbolic, official head of state. Two political parties dominate the political arena, and each has constituents from all parts of the country's heterogeneous population.

Belize is currently struggling with a major economic

overhaul.

Dependent upon old economic staples (sugar cane, agriculture and timber), Belize's economy has been stagnant, out of step with world economic trends.

Looking around the Caribbean, Belize's leadership observed how neighboring countries have turned tourism into a cash crop, raking in millions of dollars from Americans who come to enjoy the region's enchanting coasts and forests.

Belize also has tourist attractions: It offers some of the best diving in the world, dramatic Mayan ruins in the jungle, and restaurants famed for fried chinchilla - yet, compared to its neighbors, it has yet to make the grade in tourism.

Belize has recently taken steps to re-build its economy by featuring what its officials call 'ecological tourism.' Thus far, the success of the campaign has been limited. Though attractions in Belize can be more easily found today in travel brochures, the publicity hasn't jump-started the economy.

Per capita GNP is $2,300, and the country suffers from chronically high inflation.

Belize is not home to any Arab or Muslim cultural facility. The country's first mosque was built just a few years ago – and Arab immigrants weren't responsible for its construction.

The mosque was built by native Belize citizens, many of them blacks, who spent some years in the United States, converted to Islam, and then returned to their home country.

Firmly rooted in Belize

It was Palestinian Authority Chairman Yasser Arafat

who put Belize on the map of the Israeli-Palestinian dispute.

In a meeting with Israeli journalists five months ago in Ramallah, Arafat brought up the right of return issue, and alluded to Assad Shoman as an example of a person who has Palestinian roots, yet who is hardly likely to ask to redeem a right of return.

Using the Belize example, Arafat didn't get all of the facts straight. He called Shoman the prime minister of Belize, and described him as a wealthy magnate. Yet the PA chairman was right about the main point: Shoman does not intend to cash in on a right of return.

Shoman, 58, shrugs off the inaccuracies in Arafat's reference with a sense of humor. He has a soft spot in his heart for the Palestinian cause; he has even met with Arafat a number of times, coming away with a strong, positive impression regarding the Palestinian leader's skills and personality. Shoman supports Palestinian demands for an independent state, and a recognized right of return for refugees.

Yet, despite Shoman's sympathy for the Palestinian struggle, Arafat has reason not to view the Belize ambassador as a model Palestinian refugee. Cutting a striking, colorful figure - half Latin American and half Oxford English - the trained lawyer-cum-diplomat does his utmost not to be identified as a Palestinian.

'I come from there,' Shoman says, referring to the Palestinian territories. 'But I was born in Belize, to a Palestinian father and a mother with Mayan roots.'

Speaking about his childhood, Shoman suggests that he was most strongly influenced by his mother's Mayan heritage, not by his father's Palestinian culture. He doesn't know how his father wandered to Central America; nor does he know anything about the circumstances in which his father left his native home.

'Unfortunately, I didn't know anything about my father's origins until I became an adult,' Belize's High

Commissioner in the United Kingdom explains. 'My father died more than 30 years ago without saying much about his past in Palestine.'

Beyond his premier diplomatic role in Belize, Shoman is also the country's foremost historian, having written the most important record of its past.

In his history of Belize, Shoman analyzes the factors which influenced the development of the young state: British colonialism, slavery, worker disputes and the territorial conflict with Guatemala.

Though he regards immigration as a key factor in Belize's growth, Shoman does not ascribe much importance to the Palestinian immigrants, who were never more than a tiny fraction of the pool of newcomers to the state.

Though he never knew much about his father's own background, Shoman displayed interest in Palestinian issues early in his public career. In 1964 he traveled by ship with family members to Haifa. The aim of the visit was to visit Christian holy sites, but he also wanted to see where his father grew up.

When he visited Beit Hanina, Shoman discovered that many local residents had vivid memories about parts of his family history which were unknown to him.

Residents explained that his father came from one of Beit Hanina's leading families; they showed Shoman the house where his father had lived. They were also eager to hear about the Shoman family's adventures and achievements in Central America.

Shoman promised his Beit Hanina hosts that he would return, but the follow-up trip was delayed until 1973. 'The situation changed after the [1967] conquest,' he explains. 'People in the village lived under harsh conditions – the conquest was far from a pleasant experience.'

Pro-Palestinian sentiment

Shoman has formulated a clear stance on the Palestinian refugee return issue: 'The principle is that every person has a right to return to the home from which he was expelled,' he says.

But when it comes to himself and his family, Shoman emphasizes: 'I don't dream about returning there. I am a Belizean, not a Palestinian. I am a Palestinian only in terms of my origins.'

Thus, the man chosen by Arafat as an exemplification of a Palestinian exile who is successfully settled abroad, sums up his self-perception with disavowal of an active identification with the Palestinian nation.

In any case, it bears mention that a recognized right of return would, in all likelihood, not be applicable to Shoman, since he himself was not forced to depart the territories.

Shoman says he does not understand why a right of return should provoke fears. 'Belize is paradise for immigrants,' he says. 'We adopt a policy marked by care and equality, and immigrants become full citizens who contribute to the country.'

Some 40,000 immigrants have settled in Belize over the past 20 years (since the early 1980s), in a country whose population barely exceeds 200,000.

Shoman's views on the Israeli-Palestinian conflict are echoed by other members of Belize's ruling elite who have Palestinian origins.

Articulating support for Palestinian statehood demands, these Caribbean officials do not make the Palestinian struggle the paramount issue in their public activities.

In UN votes and in other international forums, Belize adopts a consistent, pro-Palestinian position; yet its diplomats do not walk the extra mile to assist the Palestinian Authority, or to sponsor international initiatives on behalf of the Palestinian people.

Though the country has a prime minister with

Palestinian roots, and also has a significant community of immigrants from Lebanon, the Palestinian issue is not on the public agenda. It isn't a hot item in the print media, nor does it play a major role in Belize's foreign policy.

Prime Minister Musa emphasizes that 'Friendship with Israel is important to us. Though we back the Palestinian people's right to an independent state, and believe that the refugees ought to be returned to their homes, we definitely support Israel's right to survive with security.'

A familiar political pattern in immigrant societies accounts partly for the Belize prime minister's formally sympathetic, yet detached, attitude on the Palestinian question.

As in other immigrant countries, politicians in Belize prefer to highlight their local roots, and keep some distance from the foreign ties left by their parents.

In conversations, both Shoman and Musa repeatedly emphasize that they are Belizeans. True, their fathers lived in Palestine and were forced to leave; but this fact, they say, doesn't alter their identities.

Shoman insists that 'The conflict in the Middle East can be solved via negotiations, because a settlement is in the interest of both sides.'

He himself is engaged in a diplomatic negotiation process, one that is also protracted though rather less acrimonious than the Middle East dispute: Shoman heads Belize's team in negotiations with Guatemala that are designed to resolve the border dispute between the two countries.

These negotiations are conducted under the auspices of the Washington-based Organization of American States (OAS).

The dignified OAS building, located in the heart of the U.S. capital, projects a sense of respectable Old World diplomacy. Negotiators smoke, saunter endlessly up and down the corridors, and break off talks in the afternoon for a mandatory two hour siesta. But, despite this calm, reputable veneer, the Belize-Guatemala dispute is a contentious topic.

Guatemala has never recognized Belize's borders, and before Belize attained independence, Guatemala even threatened to invade its territory.

The dispute flared again after several incidents in which Guatemalan residents crossed the border, and settled in relatively lucrative regions of Belize.

To phrase the issue in idiom borrowed from the Israeli-Palestinian dispute, Guatemala's aspiration is to annex these settlements in Belize. For its part, Belize demands that the internationally recognized border with its neighbor be honored.

Lisa Shoman, Assad Shoman's niece, also participates in OAS talks about the Guatemala-Belize dispute, as a member of Belize's negotiation team.

Belize's ambassador to the U.S., Lisa Shoman is younger than her uncle, and her connection with the Palestinians is even more tenuous.

One of her grandfathers (Assad Shoman's father) came from Beit Hanina, but she has never visited the territories. Yet Shoman makes a point of saying that she follows developments in the Palestinian struggle, and supports Palestinian statehood. She notes that she has not yet had an opportunity to work on Palestinian issues in the diplomatic arena; when the matter comes up, she repeats, she'll support the Palestinian right to a state.

Both Prime Minister Musa and diplomat-historian Assad Shoman view the Middle East from a distance, through Caribbean-tinted lenses.

They believe that the handling of the Belize-Guatemala dispute can be a model for negotiators in the Middle East. As they see it, hostility between Belize and Guatemala has not abated; there are some historic grudges (Belize officials charge that Guatemala's refusal to recognize its borders delayed attainment of independence from Britain for years), and there is no shortage of local clashes which harbor a potential for violent explosion.

However, Musa and Shoman explain, the dispute has never produced a major conflagration, and for dozens of years, it has been placably mediated in appropriate international forums. War, conquest and intifada are, thus, not part of the lexicon of the Caribbean dispute.

'We believe in dialogue, and can continue with it for years without resorting to weapons, hoping that a peaceful solution can be found in the future,' Musa declares.

He adds that though he would be pleased to propose the Guatemala-Belize formula as an antidote for Israeli-Palestinian woes, he has no plans for a trip to the Middle East in the near future.

'Chairman Arafat has invited me several times to visit him in Ramallah, and to see El Bireh again. But from what I read in the newspapers, this isn't exactly a good time to go to those places,' the prime minister says, speaking in an apologetic tone." – (Nathan Guttman, "From El Bireh to Belize," in *Harretz*, daily newspaper, Dallas, Texas, USA, 2001).

Belize is indeed a mixture and a blend of many groups and cultures – including immigrants – even if it's not really a melting port.

But although Belize is not a melting pot, it's home to all these groups who have blended to form a nation characterised by a wide diversity of cultures, traditions and beliefs which co-exist in relative harmony.

The vast majority of the immigrants no longer have direct ties to their ancestral homes, countries where their parents, grandparents and great-grandparents came from. They're Belizean more than anything else. In fact, the majority of them will probably tell you that they're just Belizean, and nothing else.

The Belizean society also exemplifies the preservation of individual identities and ethnic differences in spite of all the intermingling that has taken place through the years, if not centuries, since the country was founded in the 17th century. Distinct groups do exist. And they do have their own identities in terms of culture and heritage which does not compromise their collective national identity.

Although the largest ethnic group comprises people of Spanish origin – followed by the Kriol, the second-largest, and then the Garifuna and the Maya in that order – there have been some disputes over statistics in terms of how many people are in each group.

But there is no question that the demographic composition of Belize is well-defined and demarcated along ethnic lines.

According to census figures of 2000, the Mestizo constituted 48.7 per cent of the population; the Creole, 24.9 per cent; and the Garifuna, 6.1 per cent. Other groups made up 9.7 per cent of the country's population.

But these group identities are also a complex phenomenon in which a number of factors such as race, culture, language, history and heritage have together played a role in shaping them.

Therefore ethnic identity in the Belizean context is not defined purely in terms of race even though race is one of the primary factors in the equation. For example, it's not be possible to dismiss race as a factor when one talks about black Belizeans who have a distinct African heritage as one of the attributes of their ethnicity or ethnic identity different from those of other Belizeans.

There has also been some kind of re-definition of the term "black" since 1980.

The 1980 census put in the same racial category people who had earlier been identified as black and light-complexioned, the latter arbitrarily determined as black regardless of how little African they had.

This re-definition or re-classification has had a profound effect on ethnic balance in Belize. The number of Creoles has gone up sharply. Also, the Creole community has acquired another characteristic as a very diverse group in terms of physical features or characteristics.

Then there is the "caste system" based on skin colour and other physical features which, although not as prevalent in Belize as it is in the Caribbean islands, determines the fate of many Creoles within their own community – as well as outside this group.

There is racism among the Creoles themselves. Skin colour – which comes in different shades – as well as hair texture and other features can be a passport to success if you have a light complexion, straight or wavy hair or Caucasian features. The opposite is true if you have "typical" African features.

Independence has meant absolutely nothing in terms of changing such attitudes in spite of the fact that a large number of black Belizeans played a major role in the anti-colonial struggle and helped their country attain sovereign status.

The prominent role they played in the independence movement can also be partly attributed to their history of oppression as descendants of African slaves yearning to be free.

Since the era of slavery, they had – probably more than anybody else – a burning desire to be free which they radicalised into nationalist aspirations. And there was nothing that could suppress this nationalist impulse.

And in spite of the "racial differences" which exist among them as a group, they have often rallied around a common cause whenever their interests as a Creole community are threatened.

The Mestizo, who are called "Spanish" by the Creole and others, also have racial categories within their own community. But the differences in physical features among them – a product of intermarriage between the Spanish settlers and the Maya – are not as extensive as they are in the Creole community.

The Maya, who constitute the third-largest group after

107

the Mestizo and the Creole, actually belong to three separate groups – the Yucatecan, Mopán, and Kekchí Maya – even though they are identified as one people. But it's an identity that helps to reinforce their status as an indigenous people when people talk about the Maya civilisation and the Maya people.

The fourth-largest group, the Garifuna, have distinct African features although they also have Amerindian heritage as a result of intermarriage between African slaves and the Carib natives of the eastern Caribbean islands.

Among the smaller ethnic groups, East Indians constitute the largest community in Belize.

All these people live in different parts of the country including rural areas. The exception is the Chinese and Arabs, the smallest ethnic groups, who live exclusively in towns where they own shops and other businesses. Most of the Chinese live in Belize City. Arabs are found mostly in Belize and Cayo districts.

Most of the Arabs are of Palestinian origin although they also called Syrians, Lebanese and Turks.

The Chinese community grew significantly in the 1980s when large numbers of immigrants from Hong Kong and Taiwan settled in Belize. The increase in the Chinese population also accentuated cleavages, especially between the Chinese and the Creole in Belize City where many Creoles feel that they are being marginalised by the new immigrants including the Mestizo.

Mennonites, who speak German, have a unique history among immigrants in Belize because of the special status they were accorded by the government.

They were given full autonomy over their communities, becoming autonomous entities under a unitary state. Belize is not a federation or a confederation but a highly centralised state.

The Mennonites established many settlements in the Orange Walk, Cayo, and Toledo districts. And in spite of their way of life as a separate community living in their own ethnic enclaves, many Mennonites have gradually entered the mainstream, especially in the economic arena, where they work with other Belizeans.

The Mennonites of Spanish Lookout in Cayo District and Blue Creek in Orange Walk District have played a significant role in the economy as a source of dairy products and furniture. But they have invoked their religious religious rights, exempting them from military service.

In addition to the Mennonites, the only other significant group of white Belizeans are British.

But they are all a very small minority. Belize never had a large community of white settlers like Jamaica, Barbados and other island nations in the Caribbean.

The demographic profile of Belize is virtually synonymous with regional identity, an identity that is also cultural as much as it is geographic.

Most of the Creoles live in Belize City and in the areas around it where they constitute a formidable 75 per cent of the population. Belize District is their home as has been the case since colonial times. But they also live in other districts although in much smaller numbers.

Mestizos live mostly in the north and northwest in Orange Walk and Corozal districts where they constitute two-thirds of the population. They also make up 50 per cent of the population in Cayo District in the western part of the country, and about one-tenth of the population in Belize, Stann Creek, and Toledo districts.

The Garifuna live mostly along the coast in the two southernmost districts of Stann Creek and Toledo. They are a small minority in the other districts.

The majority of the Maya live in Toledo District where they constitute 57 per cent of the population. They also live in Stann Creek, Orange Walk, and Corozal districts, mostly in the rural areas as they in Toledo District.

Little has changed in these demographic patterns

through the years.

And in spite of the harmony that exists among the different ethnic and cultural groups, there have been complaints about discrimination against some groups, for example blacks and descendants of Mayans.

Some of the most vocal complaints come from blacks who contend that they are being marginalised, in spite of the fact that to some extent such "marginalisation" is the fault of black Belizeans themselves.

This "maginalisation" is attributed to the emigration of many blacks who have decided to leave Belize and go to other countries, especially the United States, thus reducing the number of black Belizeans who once were the largest group in in the country.

Nevertheless, complaints by many blacks continue and have been vociferously made even as late as 2009 by some black Belizeans such as Wellington C. Ramos, although his definition of "black" which includes East Indians is confusing. East Indians are not of African origin like the Creole and the Garifuna.

Wellington Ramos was born in Dangriga Town which is considered to be the cultural capital of Belize and specialised in urban studies. He obtained a master's degree in urban studies from Long Island University in the United States. As he stated in his commentary, "If Article 7 Is Not Passed Then Black Belizeans' Future Will Be Further Doomed," published in *Caribbean Net News*, 8 August 2009:

"Over the years, the black population in Belize has tremendously declined while the Mestizos, Chinese and other ethnic groups have increased. The black people in Belize are Creoles, Garifuna and East Indians.

The relationship among these three ethnic groups to set goals, agendas, objectives and monitor the policies of the past and present government and the impact it has on their peoples' political, economic and social living conditions is non-existent.

In fact, the relationship between the Creoles and the Garifuna people has improved but not to the point where these two largest black ethnic groups come to the realization that for them to survive in Belize, they must develop closer ties and have programs in place to address the needs and concerns of their people.

The Arab population in Belize is not large but yet, despite their small numbers, they have major political power in the country of Belize because of the amount of money that they have to throw at the poor black Belizeans and get involved in politics and win elections. Political and economic power by any group could be to the disadvantage of the other groups that are economically and politically disadvantaged.

The black Belizeans are not economically well off and this is the main reason why they migrate from Belize in large numbers to seek a better way of life in the United States. The more they migrate, the smaller their numbers become in Belize.

While their numbers are declining, the other ethnic groups are gaining in numbers and are assuming full economic and political control of the country.

Some black Belizeans are aware of this and are staying to fight against this and I applaud them for their efforts. Others believe that the only way to fight is to come to the United States, further their education and improve their economic standing, and then go home and fight for their people.

This is the reason why it is now important for the black Belizean population to support this Article 7 amendment to our constitution because it will be to their own benefit in the longer run.

Almost 95 percent of the black families in Belize have a relative in the United States that they depend on for some form of assistance. This is not the same for the Mestizos, Chinese, Mennonites, Arabs and the other ethnic groups in Belize. Most of them are doing well economically and see no need to come to the United States and live.

As an Urban Studies scholar, I have examined the wider implications of this whole amendment and the problems that will arise in the near future for the black population of Belize, if they fail to analyze the long term impact of this landmark amendment to our constitution.

There are many Belizeans who might have seen this same thing but for some strange reason are afraid to raise their voices and speak their minds. This is the time for black Belizeans who have backbones, to stand up and speak out on behalf of this injustice that has been in our constitution from the time we were given independence by Great Britain.

After all, if there is a problem with our country, we will need all the black Belizeans in the United States to come to our rescue.

There will be some who will say that this article is racist and it will further divide our people. This is far from the truth and it is only written to enlighten our people about the injustices that occur in our country every day and nothing is done about it.

The people that are opposing this amendment, are working for the very same people who are suppressing them in Belize and want to see them remain disenfranchised and keep on living in a state of poverty.

I believe that, if we had a direct vote for the election of the prime minister for Belize, Dean Barrow would not have become our first black prime minister. He is there because of the type of political system we have in Belize, where the leader of the party that wins the most seats in the House of Representatives becomes the prime minister after the elections.

For those who are thinking about amending the constitution to elect our prime minister through a direct vote they better bear this fact in their minds.

When all these consultations are completed, it will still be left to the prime minister of our country, the Right Honorable Dean Barrow, and the members of his party to proceed with this amendment where they have more than enough votes to pass it.

These consultations that are occurring are just a required part of the process before the amendments are tabled and put to a vote.

I hereby urge the prime minister to proceed without any fear because he has the support of most of the Belizeans who live in the United States and the long term rewards to his party will be substantial. After passage, the United Democratic Party will always be seen in the eyes of most Belizean Americans as the party that was there for them when they needed their support.

The People's United Party has demonstrated time and over again that they are not serving in the best interest of the Belizeans who live in the United States and abroad. They want us to continue living in a state of poverty and remain beggars for the rest of our lives while they exploit Belize for their families and themselves.

I came from a family that emphasized hard work and education like many other Belizeans that I know and we do not intend to continue living in a state of poverty.

This amendment will pass and the People's United Party will take it to the courts but hopefully by that time, the final decision will be left up to the Caribbean Court of Justice (CCJ) in the Caribbean.

Like Belize, there are other Caribbean countries who are engaging in this same political debate but their intention is to engage in a political ploy to regain control of their governments through a power grab."

Yet, there is no question that although racism exists, black people in Belize in general are better off than the indigenous people.

We are going to look at the people who make up Belize

as a nation in much more detail. And we are going to start with the Kriol who were among the first people to lay the foundation of the country when they worked as slaves.

It's not an overstatement to state that without the labour of African slaves, the British settlement in the area that came to be known as British Honduras and finally Belize would probably not have survived. And there probably would be no nation we call Belize today.

Therefore what is known as the country and nation of Belize today owes its existence, and in fact its very founding and survival, to the labour of African slaves whose descendants are known as Creoles or Kriols in Belize today.

Creoles or Kriols

Creoles or Kriols are the most influential ethnic group in Belize. And until the early 1990s, they were also the largest. The influx of immigrants form other parts of Central America into Belize in the 1980s erased this numerical superiority. Creoles are now the second-largest group in the country, after Mestizos.

Although Creoles have now been surpassed by Mestizos, they're still the most influential group in Belize. This disproportionate influence has been a source of tension between Creoles and members of other groups.

But there is also some confusion on who and what a Creole really is in the Belizean context. Many Creoles in Belize are black. A significant number of them emphasise race or racial identity when they define a Creole, clearly demonstrated by their identification with Africa and pride in their African heritage.

Yet, for practical purposes, the term "Creole" or "Kriol" has a social definition. It's also a biological definition in terms of racial identity – and identification with black Africa where African slaves came from – but it is the cultural component that carries more weight. Many Creoles have a very light complexion. Some look white and are more European than African in terms of genes. Yet they are identified as Creole because of their cultural roots and identity shaped by history.

The Creole culture in Belize is a product of Africa and Europe, a result of inter-racial relationships between the British settlers and African slaves.

The people of African descent in Belize who are identified as Creole came straight from Africa as slaves. Some of them came from the Caribbean islands, especially Jamaica, where a large number of African slaves were taken.

It is these people – the descendants of Africans and the British – who were responsible for the creation of a culture that is identified with the Creole community in Belize.

Therefore a Creole in Belize, regardless of complexion or racial identity, is identified on the basis of his or her culture and way of life, not on the basis of biological characteristics and physical appearance; although many Belizeans with distinct African features also add a racial component to the definition and even emphasise the racial aspect of Creole identity as being more important than the cultural one, as their identification with Africa and other blacks of African origin in the Caribbean islands clearly shows.

Although, in terms of race, the definition of Creole means African identity, it clearly includes customs and traditions of Anglo-Saxon origin brought to Belize by the British settlers. The definition also definitely excludes Mayan and Spanish identity and cultural values.

But apart from racial identification, many black Creoles in Belize also emphasise values which are unique to them. Some of these values are shared with blacks in the island nations of the Caribbean with whom Creoles in Belize strongly identify for racial, cultural and historical reasons including contemporary similarities derived from their common experience as descendants of African slaves and as former British subjects.

Among all the non-white groups in Belize, it is the Creole who have influenced the country the most because of their numerical preponderance through the years until they were surpassed by the Mestizos in the early 1990s. Even the dominant language of Belize is Kriol, in spite of the fact that English is the country's official language which is also taught in all schools.

Creoles work in many areas. But they dominate the civil service. And they have been accused of practising racial discrimination against other groups, especially the indigenous Maya or Mayans. According to a report, "Racism as Practiced in Belize!":

"Racism in Belize is not what you would expect after hearing stories from Europe and North America. Racism in Belize is practiced against new Chinese immigrants and the ancient Maya, who have lived on this land for more than 10,000 years.

Racism in Belize is practiced by Creoles. Mostly from the largest port town in the country, that was once the old colonial capital.

Creoles are people who are of African American descent and in Belize mostly are descended from Jamaican British West Indian Regiments that were brought into the old colony of British Honduras by logwood cutters during the era of exporting logwood trees for the dye industrialization in England and Europe in the mid 1800's to conquer the resident Maya.

These Creoles were free Black African/Jamaican soldiers in uniform under British officers of the aristocracy and commercial autocracy of England. They stayed in British Honduras and multiplied.

Since self-government these town Creoles have controlled and dominated the political format of the new nation of Belize and made sure that the treasury, the police, the Belize Defense Force and all the political power in the new nation of Belize stays in their hands.

For the past forty years these town Creoles have politically sucked 80% of the revenue of the nation collected by the government under their control and spent it on their beloved old colonial capital. In the process, they have cheated, lied and treated as second class citizens, the Mayan population, whose land they have stolen under British rule.

The worst cases of subjugation have been the southern areas of Belize and somewhat in the Western districts. Under one pretext or another, they continue to plunder the six districts comprising the new nation of Belize for their own benefit like a feudal plantation." – (Belize Development Trust, "Racism as Practiced in Belize!," Report No. 360, August, 2000).

Such accusations of racism don't seem to reflect the true image of Belize as a society where members of different racial and ethno-cultural groups live together in relative harmony. But such problems do exist. And all groups, including the Creole, have their own complaints.

It's not uncommon to hear Creoles, especially those with distinct African features, complain of racial discrimination against them by Mestizos and other Belizeans including immigrants from Asia as well as the United States.

It's true that Creoles are not the only true Belizeans. But their claim as true Belizeans is based on history and their contribution – through the centuries – to the evolution of what later became the country and the nation of Belize.

In terms of culture, their contribution is enormous. Belize culture is Kriol culture. Even the national language is Kriol although standard English is the official language. But the vast majority of Belizeans speak Kriol which is the language of the Creoles or Kriols.

Creoles have also contributed a lot in terms of food. Rice and beans is basically a Creole dish. It's the most popular dish in Belize and has its roots in Africa, especially West Africa where the majority of the slaves came from.

In fact, beans and rice is also one of the most common dishes in Black Africa south of the Sahara desert.

The history of the Creole in Belize has also been a history of suffering especially during slavery and even after slavery ended. It's also inextricably linked with the history of African slaves in the island nations of the Caribbean.

British settlers in what is now Belize began bringing African slaves in 1724. These slaves had already spent some time in Jamaica and on the Miskito Coast of Nicaragua. And there were others who came from other parts of the Caribbean.

African slaves in the area that became Belize led a better life than their brethren in Jamaica and other parts of the Caribbean. But they were still mistreated. They were even raped and killed. And they were bullied constantly by their white masters.

It is a history of suffering many of them have not forgotten just as the Maya have not forgotten theirs. Both suffered brutal treatment at the hands of their white masters.

Yet in spite of all this abuse, African slaves played a major role in defending the British settlement of Belize when it was threatened by the Spanish conquistadors in the region, especially in the latter part of the 18th century.

Their most spectacular contribution was during the Battle of St. George's Caye in 1798 when Spanish invaders from neighbouring Mexico were defeated. It was the last major battle between the British and the Spanish. And it is clear that the British would not have won the war without the help of African slaves who proved to be excellent fighters. Many of them were already excellent gunners.

The presence of African slaves in what is now Belize also led to inter-racial relationships between white men and black women. The British colony was founded by men and most of them did not have women. They ended up taking female African slaves as their mates, an intermingling which led to the emergence of another ethnic group, the Kriol, who constituted the majority of the population.

Until 1981 when British Honduras won independence and came to be known as Belize, the Kriol constituted a formidable 60 per cent of the country's population.

This racial intermingling has also caused some confusion in terms of racial identification and definition of the term "Creole"or "Kriol," even among some people in Belize, and not only among foreigners. Simply because a person has a little African blood does not mean that he or she is African. That person is no more African than a black person who has little European blood is European.

It's true that the term "Kriol" - or Creole – means more than race in the Kriol community and in the context of Belize. It's also true that the term no longer denotes purely physical characteristics or necessarily a higher percentage of African blood.

It's equally true that there are people who are mostly white, and look white, who are Kriol in terms of identity and ethnicity. Thus, it's not uncommon to see people with typical Caucasian features who are identified as Kriol – and who identify themselves as Kriol.

Kriol identity has a cultural dimension and the term "Kriol" has acquired broader meaning to denote culture as well, an identity that goes beyond physical appearance.

But that does not mean all Creoles in Belize accept this definition.

Even in the minds of many Belizeans, the racial – African – aspect of Creole identity is more important in terms of who and what a Creole really is. For example, few of them would say the first Prime Minister of Belize,

George Price, was African simply because he was Creole. He was more European than African and could not even pass for a black person if he wanted to.

Kriol identity in Belize also has a strong linguistic component. During the early years and throughout much of the country's history, the Kriol language was spoken almost exclusively by the people who identified themselves as Kriol. They were a people with their own ethnic identity and their own language – a dialect of English. Now this ethnicity has become synonymous with the Belizean national identity, especially in terms of language and even culture. It also explains why about 75 of the people in Belize speak Kriol.

And although the Kriol live mostly in Belize City, they're also found in other parts of the country, mostly in coastal and central towns and villages. Still, they are mostly identified with Belize City. Many Kriols also live in the Belize River Valley.

The ones born in Belize during the early years and in the following decades had a clear line of ancestry as a product of unions between the British as well as Scottish men and African women. But later, some other blood, including Mayan and Mestizo, also found its way into the Kriol bloodstream because of racial intermingling.

Among the Kriols of Belize are also smaller groups from other parts. These include Creoles and the Miskito from Nicaragua, besides Jamaicans and other people from different parts of the Caribbean. They all came during the early years and worked as cutters of logwood and mahogany for their white masters in the British colony which formed the nucleus of what later became British Honduras and now Belize.

And in spite of their different origins – although they were mostly black African but also from different parts of the Caribbean when they were taken to Belize – they successfully merged and formed a unique group and one of the most dynamic in Belize and in the entire Central

America.

And their language, apart from being known as Kriol, is also called Belizean Creole to distinguish it from other varieties of Creole languages spoken in different parts of the Caribbean. It also has its own unique features.

Belizean Creole, known as Kriol by its speakers, is an English Creole most closely related to Miskito Coastal Creole of Nicaragua, unlike other Creole variations in the Caribbean. But there are still similarities among them because of English being the main language common to all. Belizean Creole is also spoken by the large immigrant community of Belizeans in the United States.

It also has strong African roots, mostly from the Akan, Igbo and Twi languages of West Africa, thus providing strong evidence of where a very large number of the African slaves who originally spoke Kriol came from: Ghana (Akan and Twi) and Nigeria (Igbo), although large numbers of them also came from other parts of West Africa as well as other parts of the continent.

The prominence of Kriols in Belize was also demonstrated during the struggle of independence. The independence movement was led by a Kriol, George Price, who became the first prime minister of Belize when the country won independence from Britain. His identity as a Kriol also demonstrated another very important aspect of Kriol identity. Although a Kriol, Price was mostly white and was therefore a Kriol mostly in terms of cultural identity.

Creoles or Kriols are still prominent in Belizean society. But their numbers have dropped dramatically in sharp contrast with the numerical superiority they enjoyed until the early 1980s.

And while it's true that the influx of refugees from other Central American countries in turmoil, especially during the 1980s, and the emigration of Kriols going mostly to the United States, contributed substantially to this major demographic change to the detriment of the

Kriol community in Belize in terms of declining power and influence; it's equally true that this shift has also contributed to ethnic tensions, a troubling development in this relatively peaceful nation.

The biggest complaints come from the Kriol, some of whom invoke race to promote their agenda and portray themselves as victims of racism practised by the new immigrants from other parts of Central America as well as others.

It's a fortress mentality often justified in terms of survival and inexorably leads to demands such as "close the border." And as Guyanese Professor Ralph Premdas stated in his paper "Belize: Identity and Ethnicity in a Multi-Ethnic State," at a conference at the University of the West Indies, Cave Hill, Barbados, November 2001:

"The border with Guatemala is 266 kilometers long through which a stream of illegal immigrants and refugees have poured coming not only from Guatemala but other Central American countries such as El Salvador and Honduras especially since the early 1980s when these countries were experiencing internal civil strife.

Belize also shares a northern border of 250 kilometers with Mexico.

It has been estimated that the number of these cross border migrants approached 60,000 in the 1990s, the equivalent of about 15 to 20% of the country's population, one in six, turning it into one of the highest percentages of illegal migrants in any country in the world.[1]

Hence, Guatemala and illegal immigrants have emerged as persistent preoccupations in the Belizean imagination often tainting politics and social institutions.

Even though Belize's population of about 250,000 by 2001 was relatively small, it was diverse, composed of ethno-cultural communities many separated by language, culture, occupation, and residence: Mestizo, Creole,

Garifuna, Maya, Chinese, Syrian-Lebanese, East Indians, and Mennonites.

Two of these communities, the Creoles and Mestizos, constitute about three fourths of the total population so that the country can be conceived as predominantly ethnically bi-polar.

By the end of WW II, the Creole ethno-cultural group was the dominant community with about 55% of the population but it was slowly diminishing so that by 1980 their numbers were about 39.7%, and by 2001, it had been reduced to just fewer than 30% while Mestizos steadily grew hovering today around or slightly exceeding 50%.

This was a dramatic re-alignment of Belize's ethnic demography stemming from the confluence of two opposite migratory flows.

Creoles who were the descendants of the African slaves brought to toil for Europeans mainly as woodcutters in the colonial period were migrating since the 1970s in large numbers to North America.

It is possible that in the 1980s as many Creoles left Belize as Central American immigrants entered the country during the same period.

The resulting impact was that the previously dominant Afro-Belizean community on whose back Belize was historically colonized was being eclipsed by a Mestizo population which was constantly being replenished by continuing cross-border refugee infusions.

I have heard said that the Creole community has become traumatized by this rather rapid fall from its ascendancy, some even claiming that they were being marginalised, even becoming the victims of a peculiar form of 'ethnocide' similar to what Aime Cesaire in Martinique described as 'genocide by substitution' referring to the heavy infusion of French Europeans into Martinique and the corresponding loss of Martiniquans to France.[2]" - (Ralph R. Premdas, "Belize: Identity and Ethnicity in a Multi-Ethnic State," a paper presented at the

Belize Country Conference, University of West Indies, Cave Hill, Barbados, 21 – 24 November 2001. See also, cited by Premdas, Joseph O. Palacio, "Social and Cultural Implication of Recent Demographic Changes in Belize", *Belizean Studies*, 21(1), 1993).

Although Kriols are the most traumatised group in this realignment of forces, tipping scales against their favour, they're still some of the most powerful people in the country.

And in spite of its broader definition that incorporates a cultural dimension, the term "Kriol" is still closely identified with "black" and has been used as a weapon by Kriol nationalists in their demand for "equality" with other groups.

But the definition can be confusing. Sometimes, it has subtle meaning.

It's confusing and subtle because while it has a racial dimension or component, it excludes some black Belizeans; which is a concession, however inadvertently, that the term is more cultural than racial by definition.

In the Belizean context, the term "Kriol" is used to identify any person of at least partial Black African descent – regardless of how little African blood he or she has – but who is *not* who Garifuna. Yet the Garifuna are also a people of African ancestry. And Creole Afrocentric advocates talk about the imperative need for unity between Creoles and Garifunas based on common bonds of shared African heritage.

The term Creole or Kriol is also further confusing because it embraces other people. Any person who speaks Kriol as a first language, or as the only language, is, by definition, a Kriol. This includes immigrants from Africa and the West Indies who have settled in Belize and have intermarried with local people.

In fact, the concept of Kriol and that of "mixture" have almost become synonymous to the extent that any

124

individual with Afro-European ancestry combined with any other ethnicity – whether Mestizo, Garifuna or Maya – is now likely to be considered "Kriol." An as Michael A. Camille states in *Belize: Selected Proceedings from the Second Interdisciplinary Conference*:

"The designation 'Creole' has a different meaning (in Belize) than it does in some other Caribbean countries.

In Belize, a Creole refers to a person with a significant percentage of black blood. Thus, the usage of Creole is similar to that of 'mulatto' in the Caribbean." – (Michael A. Camille, in Michael D. Phillips, ed., *Belize: Selected Proceedings from the Second Interdisciplinary Conference*, Lanham, Maryland, USA: University Press of America, 1996, p. 47).

The difference is rooted in history and in the different social dynamics which have shaped Belizean society in spite of the fact that it's considered to be a part of the Caribbean Anglophone community of nations although it's a Central American nation.

And although the history of the Kriol is inextricably linked with the history of Belize Town, now Belize City, as their original and main settlement, their logwood settlements along the banks of the Belize River were almost equally important. They were also business settlements involving fishing and logwood cutting.

Some of the main settlements included Burrell Boom, Bermudian Landing, Crooked Tree, Gracie Rock, Rancho Dolores and Flowers Bank.

There were also substantial numbers of Kriols in and around the plantations south of Belize City at All Pines and Placencia.

As years went by, especially in the 19th century, the Kriols moved to other parts of what is now Belize, mainly Dangriga in Stann Creek District and Monkey River in Toledo District in the southern part of the country. They did so when the British settlement continued to expand, incorporating other areas into it.

They were also known for their pride in their heritage and identity. This sometimes led to conflict with their British masters, events which were a sign of things yet to come. Some of the most dramatic events included riots against the British settlers who controlled the colony.

In the 1900s, the Kriols played a major role in developing Belize. They took the lead. Then came the riots in 1919 and 1934, triggered by economic and political injustices against them.

Their predicament was compounded by the devastation wrought by a very powerful hurricane which hit British Honduras (now Belize) hard in 1931.

A combination of all those factors fuelled political agitation among the Creoles, leading to the establishment of the first trade unions in the country.

The trade unions themselves became incubators of nationalist agitation and helped in mobilising forces which led to the formation of the first political party, the People's United Party (PUP), which eventually led the country to independence.

So, from all this, it's clear that Creoles have played a central if not the dominant role in the political awakening and evolution of the country, eventually leading to the birth of the new nation of Belize; a role many Creoles believe gives them the right to be acknowledged as the founders of the nation.

By logical extension, it's an acknowledgement which some Creoles also believe entitles them to special treatment and privileges other Belizeans should not be entitled to. And that is a recipe for disaster.

Still, there is no question that Kriols have played a unique role in the development of Belize as a nation other groups have not because of historical circumstances and realities. Together with the indigenous people and the British settlers, they were among the first people to settle in Belize. No other group can claim that distinction in Belize today besides the indigenous people.

Historical forces which have shaped Belize and Creole identity can be view from another perspective, one reinforcing the mythological status of the Creole as the ones "ordained" to lead Belize. Guyanese scholar Ralph Premdas, who went on a one-month study tour of Belize in April 2001, does not specifically ascribe that status to the Creole but acknowledges their special place in Belizean history in the following terms:

"The lingua franca is Belize Creole, spoken with an accent very similar to Creolese in Guyana....

My temporary home was in Belize City, the capital, which is preponderantly populated by 'Creoles,' the local name assigned to the descendants of the African slaves who were recruited not for sugar plantations as in the insular Caribbean but for harvesting logwood, mahogany and other lumber by the British.

The British presence commenced in the mid-1600s in a region claimed by Spain and was alternatingly marked by periods of accommodation and conflict.

The final decisive attack occurred in 1798 when a numerically superior Spanish military contingent was routed by the 'Baymen' as these English settlers were called.

This has become a signal event in Belizean history around which has emerged a mythological basis for the claim of Creoles as the rightful cultural and political inheritor of Belize after the departure of the British.

The narrative depicts victory over the Spanish forces in the Battle of St. George Caye by the heroic combined effort of the enslaved African slaves and the British colonists so that Belize's status as a former British colony and today as an independent English-speaking state is due to this historic event.

The part played by the Creoles in repelling the Spanish

as it is now being recounted attests to their loyalty to Belize as an autonomous and free entity and stands as a symbol that affirms their privileged position above all other communities in the country. This mythology is backed up at the level of culture where today an adapted English culture is dominant in Belize, even though it is now highly Americanized.

The main language is English and the medium of instruction in all schools and of commerce is English. The main political institutions such as the parliamentary system are similarly of British origin. The Creoles are the main cultural carriers of this cultural inheritance while others adapt to it.

Two respected observers stated this point thus: 'Anglophone Creoles came to consider British Honduras as 'theirs', defining it as Black, Protestant, and English-speaking. In doing so, they sought to define all other ethnic groups as marginal outsiders, or 'aliens".[7]

They often parade this cultural inheritance in symbolic ways in public to assert their paramountcy.

The Creole community is replete with professionals in the areas of law, medicine, education, the public service, etc (but not business and commerce) and there is a well-off Creole elite, many mixed with European ancestry and of light pigmentation, locally referred to as 'the Royal Creoles.'

Many Creoles regard themselves are socially superior in status to members of other communities which have had to acculturate to English ways.

While their cultural standing has been maintained, the same has not been the case in the political realm because of their diminished numbers. In Belize City, however, they remain dominant but even this is being restructured with the entry of many Central American 'aliens' into the city.

Since independence in 1981, there has never been a Creole Prime Minister even though they have occupied powerful cabinet posts and other positions of power. One of the two major political parties in Belize, the United Democratic Party (UDP) is seen by many as grounded in the Creole community presently led by Dean Barrow, from a 'Royal Creole' pedigree.

It has been remarked to me more than once that Dean Barrow as the Leader of Opposition in the Parliament would never be able to become Prime Minister of Belize since he was Creole (when Professor Premdas wrote this essay in 2001, Barrow was still the opposition leader but he became prime minister about 7 years later in 2008, the first black to reach the highest office in the land, two years before I wrote this book – update by Godfrey Mwakikagile)." – (Ralph Premdas, "Belize: Identity and Ethnicity in A Multi-Ethnic State," op.cit. See also, cited by Premdas, Nigel Bolland and Mark Moberg, "Development and National Identity: Creolisation, Immigration, and Ethnic Conflict in Belize," *International Journal of Comparative Race and Ethnic Studies*, 2: 1995, pp. 1-18).

The legitimacy of the claim that Creoles – or Kriols – are the only true Belizeans has been seriously contested by other ethno-cultural and racial groups in Belize. And it faces challenges in the future if Creoles attempt to use it as an entitlement which gives them the right to enjoy a privileged status in a multi-ethnic and multi-cultural society.

Also, black identity politics has failed to mobilise and draw a large number of Creoles in pursuit of a political agenda based on race. One of the main reasons for this failure is that Creole identity – which incorporates other elements besides black African heritage – is, by definition, a cultural phenomenon more than anything else.

This does not mean that Creoles don't have legitimate claims or grievances when some of them complain about racism. As descendants of a people who have suffered discrimination from the beginning when Belize was founded as a country, it is difficult to believe that even under the best of circumstances, they no longer suffer discrimination.

There are many times when black people in Belize suffer discrimination even if for no other reason than that they're members of what may be the most despised race on earth who are not accepted by other people as equals; with their black identity being seen by many non-blacks as badge of inferiority.

Even among the Creole themselves, there are "racial divisions" or gradations of race.

The preference of a light complexion over a dark complexion is just one example of the burden of colour. It demonstrates that blacks are still considered inferior regardless of how successful they are in life. The darker, the uglier; the lighter, the prettier.

The colour problem also extends to the intellect, a situation analogous to the status of Africa as "the dark continent" whose people have "darkness" in their mind because they have a dark skin.

And that's just one aspect of the complexity of race and ethnicity in the Belizean context.

Therefore, even in Belize, where multicultural forces have played a major role in shaping the society, with many people identifying themselves on the basis of cultural identity more than anything else, race still matters; not only in the case of black Belizeans but of others as well, including the indigenous people, the Maya, who are the most disadvantaged group in the country. They're still powerless today in the land of their ancestors.

So, it's not really a question of whether or not racism exists in Belize. It does exist just like everywhere else. The question is how pervasive and corrosive is it in this multiracial society whose very foundation was laid by racist colonisers from Britain.

They seized the land from the indigenous people. They

abused and exploited them. The British settlers also brought African slaves to work for them. All that was racism even if the primary motive was economic.

Professor Ralph Premdas has asked and answered this question about racism in Belize in the following terms:

"Is there racism in Belize?

How has Belize like the new societies of the Caribbean fared, having traversed the terrain to decolonisation and modernity, with regard to the persistence of racism? How far has Belize proceeded in establishing a society free from ethnic and racial particularism, and based on merit or compassion?

To answer these questions, one must examine the full kaleidoscope of cultural and political forms that have emerged in the society.

Racism is an ideology that seeks to justify the skewed allocation of resources in favor of a group on the basis of alleged phenotypical and biological differences. What is critical about this definition is that one group deliberately discriminates against another using fictive differences.

Generally, ethno-cultural communities in practically all polyethnic states tend to compose their claims to a distinctive identity by attributing to themselves in their narratives of origin not only cultural and historical differences but racial myths of superiority over rival groups.

With rare exceptions, racial claims tend to be implicated in the construction of cultural identities. Some of these racial claims have tended to be quite explicit as in the old apartheid South Africa but in many others, such as Belize, the racial claims are less evident, intermixed with other factors, and frequently denied altogether.

In Belize, solidarity communities are categorized in part by their culturally constructed traits involving language, religion, region, and sectional values. This is witnessed in the sorts of biological racist terms that are often used in stereotypical portraits and abusive language employed in depicting other communities.

I have heard the word 'primitive' as well as the 'n' word used as well as references to 'whites,' 'yellows' etc. Racio-phenotypical traits are clearly implicated by the prevalence of racial slurs and invidious stereotypes in day-to-day interaction.

It is not important that racial categories are accurately described or scientifically grounded by the communities but perceived to be true becoming part of a social map that guides daily interaction.

Discrimination may not always be based exclusively on phenotype; it is often linked to and combined with other differences. In these instances, racial myths are articulated into a mix of cultural, religious, linguistic and other differences and turned into a mode defining inter-group relations.

As a result, the term *ethnic* is brought into service because of its wider scope.

Ethnicity refers to a collective sense of consciousness often constructed on racial, cultural, linguistic, religious, or regional claims so as to assert exclusive group identity against rival claims of other groups.

Race is often a component of the phenomenon of ethnicity, but is not always present or self-evident.

In the Belizean context, the racial factor is frequently implicit in ethnic group differentiation even where it would involve persons who are mixed.

Racial mixing does not produce racial tolerance but may evolve into new forms of racial-constructed categorization.

While today, the formal trappings of social differentiation and discrimination built around open racial difference have been removed, much inequality and petty oppression persist around a colour continuum.

This nuanced continuum engages many variations in colour to which, ironically, racial traits are constructed.

The practices of 'colourism' are impregnated with racial motifs which are now more likely to be manifested through subtle ways.

The historical context has changed, and the victims and victimizers are differently attired. The political, social, and economic milieux have been transformed. Basic structures of struggle in the context of scare resources and the quest for power and privileges point to a new drama in which old colonially inspired themes of distinction and discrimination are played out.

The actors in the diverse Belizean landscape are not antagonistically the same: Whites against Blacks. It is now mainly Blacks against Blacks; Blacks against browns; high browns against low browns; Africans against Indians, blacks against yellows, etc.

In Belize, as in most of the Caribbean, the actors are non-White. Nigel Bolland spoke well on this subject: arguing that this state of affairs 'is partly due to the colonial legacy of racism which discriminates particularly against people of African descent – both Creoles and Garifuna – while relatively favoring those with lighter skins and straighter hair. A light-skinned Mestizo child who learns English and attends a prestigious St.John's College is more likely to rise into the Belizean elite than a dark-skinned Creole-speaking child of African descent.'[30]

The resources for which the new racial struggle is conducted are no longer the control of the labor of non-White persons to produce sugar, tobacco, and cotton on plantations. It is now jobs, status, and privileges in a stratified order deriving its resources from multinational corporations, multilateral aid agencies, and other international sources.

The tools of control are no longer slavery and identureship, explicit laws of discrimination, residential and occupational segregation, and formal codes of deference. They are now colour prejudice, custom, cliqueism, clientelist networks, kin connections and appearance.

This is all defended by neo-racial notions of group identity and solidarity, in group behavior and communal traditions.

The overt manifestations and consequences are not always obvious. They have to be sought in the thinking, ideologies, elite structures, leadership recruitment patterns, cultural preferences, and substructural expression of the actors." – (Ralph R. Premdas, "Belize: Identity and Ethnicity in a Multi-Ethnic State, " a paper presented at the Belize Country Conference, University of West Indies, Cave Hill, Barbados, 21 – 24 November 2001.

See also, cited by Premdas, Nigel Bolland, "Ethnicity, Pluralism and Politics in Belize," in *Identity, Ethnicity, and Culture in the Caribbean* edited by Ralph R. Premdas, Trinidad:School of Continuing Studies, University of the West Indies, 2000), p. 11).

The use of nuanced arguments to justify privilege and exclusion as well as discrimination is a sophisticated form of racism, often expressed in coded language, which is an integral part of life in Belize. Even crude racism in not uncommon. The mere fact that it is denied or downplayed by many Belizeans does not mean that it does exist.

Although Creoles are some of the most outspoken people in Belize, complaining about racism, they are also accused by many non-Creoles of being some of the most racist people in the country.

It is a double-edged sword. And it cuts both ways.

Next, we look at the Garifuna as an ethnic and cultural entity in relation to other groups in Belize's multi-racial and multicultural context.

Garifunas

The Garifuna, like the Creole, trace their roots all the way back to Africa.

But unlike the Creole, the Garifuna also have indigenous roots, in the Caribbean, and celebrate this dual identity although some Creoles also have native blood – Mayan – from the racial intermarriage with the indigenous people that has taken place through the years.

And some Creoles, unlike the Garifuna, identify more with their African heritage than they do with their indigenous roots.

All this again shows the complex nature of ethnicity and ethnic identities in Belize unlike in other countries in the region including those in the Caribbean.

And the subtle distinction between the terms Garifuna and Garinagu can sometimes be confusing.

Garifuna is the singular form of Garinagu. The language is also known as Garifuna. The term Garifuna is also used to describe the culture.

Thus, the Garinagu have a Garifuna culture, while a Garifuna has Garifuna culture and speaks the Garifuna language. And the Garinagu speak Garifuna and have Garifuna culture.

The Garifuna language is a combination of Arawak and Carib with some English, French, and Spanish influences. It also has some African elements mainly from the tribes of West Africa.

And quite often, the people themselves are simply called Garifuna. In fact, many of them prefer to be called Garifuna or Garifunas, instead of Garinagu.

Their name is derived from "karifuna" which means "of the cassava clan." Cassava is very popular in all Garifuna communities where the Garifuna live – Belize, Honduras, Nicaragua, Guatemala and elsewhere – and it forms a common bond among them. It's their "national" food, uniting all Garifunas.

The Garifuna have also played an important role in shaping Belizean identity although not as much as the dominant group, the Creole, have.

In terms of cultural and racial identity the Garifuna are a product of Africa, the Caribbean and Europe. But they're mostly descendants of African slaves and Caribs, a tribe native to the islands in the West Indies after which the Caribbean region is named. They have only a small percentage of European blood in general although there are some who have more Caucasian blood than others just like many Creoles and other Belizeans do.

Their roots in the Caribbean are on the small island of St. Vincent where African slaves intermarried with the native Caribs who in a larger regional context are also known as Amerindians. The British rulers of St. Vincent called them Black Caribs to distinguish them from the native Caribs who did not intermarry with the African slaves.

It's believed that the Black Caribs – or Garifunas – first arrived in Belize, in what was then British Honduras, on 19 November 1802. It's a date and an event that is as important to the Garifuna as the landing of the *Mayflower* on Plymouth Rock is to Americans. November 19th is celebrated by the Garifuna as Settlement Day. The celebration is held in Dangriga, the Garifuna capital in southern Belize.

Settlement Day is also celebrated by other Belizeans as an integral part of their nation's multicultural identity.

When the British expelled them from St. Vincent for resisting oppression and racial injustices, little did they or the exiled Garifunas realize that this group was on its way to becoming one of the most important and most influential groups in its new home in Central America.

Today, the Garifuna constitute the third-largest ethnic group in Belize. And their influence is evident in many areas of national life, including food and music. In fact, the "national music" of Belize, punta – from which the popular Punta Rock is derived – is traditional Garifuna music. It has African roots. And some of the best cuisines

136

enjoyed by other Belizeans are Garifuna. The list goes and on.

The history of the Garifuna in Belize is inextricably linked with the southern part of the country where they established five major settlements in 1832. The region is still a Garifuna stronghold even today.

Although they live in a country whose main culture, including the language, is Kriol, the Garifuna have been able to maintain their identity as a distinct ethnic group. They have their own culture. They have their own language. They also have their own history.

It's an ethnic group which is a product of cultural fusion. It's also a group that's held together by strong traditional values including religious beliefs some of which can be traced all the way back to Africa. It also has evolved and maintained its own unique identity in the Belizean multicultural context.

But there has also been a change in the demographic pattern and composition, and life style, of the Garifuna community in Belize in recent years which can be attributed to a number of factors including economic.

Many people, especially the younger ones, have left in search of better opportunities elsewhere, leaving behind the youngest and the oldest. Here is just one example, a Garifuna community in Barranco, southern Belize, to illustrate the point. According to a case study in *Indigenous and Traditional Peoples and Protected Areas: Principles, Guidelines, and Case Studies*:

"In Barranco, economic depression has led to a steady exodus of its residents to other areas of Belize and the United States.

The Garifuna, who were traditionally expert fishermen, and also grew bananas and rice for export, found their livelihoods undermined by the 1980s with the depletion of fish stocks, the domination of the banana market by large growers and the closure of the government rice buying

137

centre.

Barranco's remaining residents now rely heavily on assistance from family members living abroad.

Although residents of Barranco are no longer as dependent on farming as they once were, they too are concerned about land invasions and their own insecure land tenure position. Like the Maya, they wish to secure legal claims to their ancestral lands, which they regard as their communal patrimony.

In recent years, Toledo's pristine resources have captured the attention of international and national developers, and the district's previous isolation is being steadily eroded." – (Javier Beltrán, ed., *Indigenous and Traditional Peoples and Protected Areas: Principles, Guidelines, and Case Studies*, Case Study 3, Island Press, 1 June 2000).

Major economic changes in any country, including loss of jobs and declining employment opportunities, tend to disrupt communities. The Garifuna community in Belize is no exception. It has come under such strain, as has the Creole community and others in the country, threatening stability and cohesion in the community.

One of the main factors which has enabled it to withstand this disruptive impact is culture and the strong values members of the community continue to cherish and implement in their lives.

It is this cultural strength and continuity that will ensure the survival of the Garifuna community as an ethnic entity with its own identity in a multicultural society.

And while the Garifuna know that they are an integral part of Belize, they are also aware of their place in society as a distinct group, a status claimed and enjoyed by other groups as well, and as a people who have made a unique contribution to the evolution and development of the nation through the years.

This distinct identity is also reinforced by geography. The areas where the vast majority of the Garifuna live in southern Belize are clearly identified as Garifuna territory. The territory is as geographical as it is ethno-cultural even if it's not necessarily identified as an ethnic enclave. And many Garifuna, including some of their leading intellectuals, have taken steps to preserve and promote their unique identity and culture in the context of Belize as a distinct group. As Professor Ralph Premdas wrote about his experience in Belize:

"While the population was ethnically diverse, Belize had a unique community of 'Garifuna,' sometimes called 'Black Caribs' who were the descendants of Caribs from the island of St. Vincent.[3]

While there were remnants of the Caribs still on the Caribbean islands, notably Dominica (4%), and St. Vincent and the Grenadines (5.3%), in contrast, Belize as well as Honduras, Guatemala and Nicaragua, had become home to a significant minority of Garifuna.[4]

Belize also had Mayas. The other parts of the Caribbean that had an aboriginal population that was akin to the Mayas and Garifuna was Guyana (6%) which had nine tribal communities and Suriname (10%).

As a whole, the remaining aboriginal groups in the Caribbean have been barely visible even though there has been an appreciable rise in their self-consciousness in the 1970s and 1980s witnessed by the formation of several representative organizations seeking recognition and economic development.[5]

I was lucky that my Belizean host was Dr.Joseph Palacio, an anthropologist who was the Resident Director of the University of West Indies Extra-mural School of continuing Studies in Belize.

With my keen interest in Belize's people, Dr. Palacio himself was a source of intrigue since he was a Garifuna with a Ph.D. from University of California at Berkeley, an institution at which I was an Assistant Professor at the beginning of my academic career.

Dr.Palacio was a 'Garifuna,' and I was of East Indian background coming originally from Guyana, the descendant of indentured laborers recruited from India for the sugar plantations after slavery was abolished.

Dr. Palacio's wife, Myrtle, was also Garifuna. Their home in Belize City was a large two-story concrete bungalow and it was a veritable museum of Garifuna art and artifacts. I was given a tour and came face to face with a civilization that had for the most part vanished from the insular Caribbean.

The Caribs, Tainos, Ciboneys and Arawaks were the First Nations of the islands and they were practically decimated with European colonization with faint echoes of their past written mockingly in contemporary names like 'Caribbean.'

In the tour of the Palacio home, there was a huge mural of a traditional Garifuna village partly portraying the process by which *ereba* (cassava bread) was produced very similar to that in Guyana among a tribal community a few miles from where I lived on the Corentyne River in an Amerindian village called Orealla.

I inquired about the Garifuna, an unfamiliar name in the Caribbean where the word 'Carib' was the familiar designation of the aboriginal inhabitants. As it turned out, the word 'Garifuna' – plural 'Garinagu' – was a terminology of recent vintage adopted only in 1975 by a group of Garifuna intellectuals including Dr. Palacio, who sought to replace the Anglophone term 'Carib' as 'a way of expressing identity in a people's own language.'[6]

In 1797, the British expelled the rebellious indigenous Caribs from St. Vincent and practically threw them to the winds dumped on Roatan island off the coast of Honduras. Against all odds, they survived, regrouped and re-settled

140

into a variety of communities throughout Central America mainly on the Caribbean coast.

The Garifuna historical memory recounts their ferocity in resisting the British and other colonizers on St. Vincent, for which they were summarily evicted en masse.

In part, the British anger against the Caribs stemmed from the fact that they offered shelter and sanctuary to escaped slaves from the regimented plantations. In due course, these 'maroons' inter-married with the Caribs so that today there is practically no 'pure' Carib alive but they have retained their cultural identity and self-definition as an aboriginal people.

They have maintained a vibrant network of communications and travel among themselves especially between Dangriga in Belize, Livingston in Guatemala, and Trujillo in Honduras. They have acculturated to the Spanish society around them many becoming Catholics, and while they have preserved old customs, they have assumed Spanish names and have adapted to Spanish culture and language throughout Central America.

Belizean Garifuna now have certain characteristic Spanish surnames such as Palacio, Hernandez, Flores, etc. And quite a few are Catholic priests and bishops.

In 1832, a number of the Garifuna came to the British colony of British Honduras (later Belize) settling in the south and gradually acculturating to English ways and language. Dr. Palacio was born in one of these first Garifuna villages, Baranco, the primordial place of his first loyalty.

Today, the Garinagu have become an integral part of the Belizean mosaic of peoples constituting about 6 to 7% of the population and strongly represented in the area of education.

Their contribution to Belize's development has been recognized on a particular day in the Belizean calendar called "Settlement Day."

A National Garifuna Council expresses and defends

their interests and several Garifuna have become members of parliament and cabinet ministers.

The Town of Dangriga in the south of the country is predominantly Garifuna.

The Garifuna in Belize have been part of a mass migration to the USA mainly to Los Angeles so that it is said that as many of them live in Belize as in other countries, mainly in North America.

Joe remarked that there was a crisis in identity for as the Garifuna migrate they lose their language and ways that make them a distinctive people.

Joseph and Myrtle and their two children have refused to leave Belize fiercely loyal to their way of life, speaking their language at home, and actively promoting Garifuna interests in Belize and everywhere they reside.

Dr. Palacio was at one time an executive member of World Council of Indigenous Peoples and has previously served as the Head of the Department of Archaeology in Belize.

Myrtle is also an accomplished person with a degree from Berkeley and currently serves as the head of Belize's Elections Commission...." (Ralph Premdas, "Belize: Identity and Ethnicity in a Multi-Ethnic State," at a conference at the University of the West Indies, Cave Hill, Barbados, November 2001).

He goes on to state:

"Dangriga, located on the coast, was a preponderantly Garifuna town with a Garifuna mayor and Garifuna members of parliament, including the Speaker of Parliament, Sylvia Flores.

Dangriga was an old fishing settlement pointing to the potential for a marine industry. This I did find, but it was not constituted of a fishing fleet but shrimp farms on land, that is, fish farms next to the coastline.

Expatriate-owned and controlled, these farms produced

6,367,886 pounds of shrimps in 2001 valued at $46,497,000 thereby making a major contribution to Belize's export sector. But they were not integrated into the Dangriga and Garifuna landscape.

Dangriga recollects some of the early strivings of the Garifuna people as they entered Belize at the southern coastal parts, setting up villages including Dangriga.

They were soon recruited thereafter by the Baymen as woodcutters joining the Creoles in this founding colonial enterprise.

But the Garifuna were also great seamen and wharf workers, a set of interrelated occupations that came to define part of their identity throughout Belize and Central America.

In Dangriga, the Garifuna had evolved further into other niches carving out a distinctive claim as educators and teachers.

In Dangriga, my host was Austin Flores, a retired High School Principal of high regard among the Garifuna. He ran a small motel located on a beachfront.

From the bus top, it was a short walk to Flores motel where I was expected and warmly greeted.

An educated, well travelled and very articulate man, Flores was also Vice-President of the National Garifuna Council.

I asked him why he did not migrate to the United States which he had visited many times and in which he had several family members, he said that he could not stand racism and preferred living in dignity in Belize.

Asked about his retirement pre-occupations, he said he was busy with his motel but also a small citrus farm. He remarked that although there was a high unemployment rate in Dangriga, the Garifuna refused to take available jobs in the banana and citrus plantations arguing that they paid too little.

He contemptuously declared that the Garifuna had abandoned village and farm life for the bright lights of

143

towns not only like Dangriga and Belize City but also Los Angeles, New York, and Chicago.

Dangriga itself was a fairly compact town with a busy and dusty main street, St. Vincent Street, closely rimmed by an assortment of shops, houses and vacant spots.

The next day, I took a walk along the main street in the direction of the river that divides the town into two sections.

Along the main road I was struck by the remnants of a number of dilapidated houses interspersed with well-stocked stores.

In particular, I was struck by a particular dilapidated house, which was partly occupied by young people drinking liquor and playing cards and dominoes.

The shops seem to be all stocked with the same plastic wares and cheap household goods and, as in Belize City, owned by Chinese business people.

To be sure, a few shops were owned by local residents and I entered one of these after seeing some sweet potato pies, a Garifuna specialty.

I struck up a conversation with the storekeeper, a middle aged woman, who told me that she was Garifuna and had migrated from Honduras to Belize. She said that the several Garifuna settlements in Central America shared a common communication grid among relatives who pass across borders frequently.

Proceeding to the river where the bridge crossed, I found a new set of riverain commercial activities both from the small boats plying the water as well from a series of shops that bordered on the confluence of the river and road. Across from the river was the fresh vegetable, fish and fruit market of Dangriga which I made a point in visiting the next morning, a Saturday, Market Day.

Like many tropical markets that I have seen around the world, this one was full of life, teeming with buyers and sellers, fruits and vegetables spread on the ground, and everyone colourfully dressed for the occasion.

144

At a section where there were quite a few small vendors plying a large variety of familiar fruit and vegetables, I saw 'ereba,' the white stiff cassava bread, for which the Caribs and other Amerindian groups in the Caribbean were famous.

Everyone seemed to know each other and there was quite a bit of socializing and revelry.

Next to the market was the river bank to which gathered a number of boats carrying vegetables and fruits from farmers from other parts of Stan Creek District. The supply was abundant and relatively inexpensive.

Mr. Flores had arranged for me to see the mayor of Dangriga, Cassian Nunez, who had returned from Los Angeles to assist in the development of Dangriga. He was most personable and like so many of the Garifuna I had met extraordinarily articulate as he painstakingly took me for a trip through the township.

He was very keen about stimulating economic development in Dangriga where the unemployment situation was serious. He saw the need to attract new investment in tourism and small manufacturing businesses as the solution to this end. He remarked that there was an acute shortage of land while simultaneously there existed very large citrus and banana plantations just outside of the town.

He was as concerned like Dr. Palacio was about the rise of drug use among the youths and said that the place along the road that I saw with many persons drinking and playing cards was a main staging area for the drug trade and criminal activities.

Crack cocaine was a critical problem in Dangriga as well as HIV-AIDS.

Along the way, I was attracted by some new construction of low cost houses which it was explained to me was part of a promise that the Prime Minister had made in the last elections to provide 200,000 such houses during his tenure.

Cassian was concerned because at mid-point in the life of the new government not much was yet done to construct enough of them. He was asked about political patronage in the construction process and he said it pervaded the entire system so that party stalwarts were the recipients of benefits. He said that was the case in everything in Belize.

At another location of the town, I saw a mass outdoor event in the making on a large football size field on which were numerous plastic chairs crowned by a stage and a podium. It was an Evangelical or Pentecostal religious revival meeting which was very popular in many parts of Central America conducted by expatriate religious groups from the USA.

The Mayor explained that the group that I saw was from Guatemala and had found fertile ground in Dangriga as in other (parts) of Belize where unemployment was high.

I asked about the Garifuna faith and its importance to the Garifuna people today. He said that many Garifuna had become Christians mainly Catholics but also many had combined their adherence to Christian rituals with the Garifuna.

I was told about the persistence of traditional 'dugu' ceremony and ancestor worship among the Garifuna suggesting that it was one of the authentic Garifuna defining practices still in existence.

Many persons I had met in Belize have told me that 'obeah' and similar spirit possession practices prevailed but that it was especially pronounced among the Garifuna. I was invited to meet a main practitioner of the *dugu* ceremony but I declined.

Mr. Flores also felt that I should meet a distinguished Garifuna couple, Eugene and Felicia Hernandez, who were also Garifuna returnees from the diaspora and who had established a home in Dangriga.

Felicia Hernandez was famous for her many books on

Garifuna folktale and children's books. I was invited to dinner and entered a very substantial but well secured bungalow attesting to widespread fear of burglary in Dangriga.

Eugene and Felicia were retired and wanted to preserve the Garifuna way of life and its historical memory.

Eugene, who was the one who insisted on returning to Belize, had taken up farming around Dangriga. Felicia reluctantly joined her husband pointing out that she was adapting to all of the inconveniences of Dangriga and was not too dissatisfied.

She had written several children's books and had etched much recognition for her work, several copies of which were given to me. They had children who continued to reside in the USA.

When I was in Belmopan, I had taken time out to see Mr. Roy Caeytano who was the current President of the National Garifuna Council. He had invited me for summer with his family at his home in Dangriga that weekend.

Cayetano was tall, trim and articulate as well as well traveled and educated with advanced university degrees. He has been a frequently invited person to international conferences on development issues.

At dinner, his teenage children and wife joined him in a Garifuna prayer of thanks. Mrs. Cayetano was also a well-educated Garifuna schoolteacher.

The home was decorated with Garifuna artifacts and paintings.

We discussed many problems of the Garifuna people of which the main one pertained to the loss of the Garifuna language and Garifuna traditions generally in part stemming from the large Garifuna diaspora.

I asked Roy about an upcoming Garifuna event sponsored by 'The World Garifuna Council' that was scheduled a month later. I was told that the event was hosted by Dr. Ted Aranda, a Garifuna member of parliament in the current government but that the event did not receive the blessing of the National Garifuna Council. Evidently, there was quite a bit of infighting among the Belize Garifuna elite and this was manifested in the event for all of the public to see" – (Ibid.).

Also, the assertion of ethnic identity has had unintended consequences, leading to competing claims among the different groups with regard to land rights, political leadership and other things including "Who is a true Belizean?"

While many people in these groups emphasise group rights, it's probably not their intention to question the existence of Belize as a multiracial and multicultural society or the legitimacy of its existence as a nation. But claims of group rights, as opposed to individual rights which is the basis of true democracy, do tend to divide the nation. And the claims are strident as ever:

"The Garifuna for example underscore that like the ancient Mayas, they are indigenous to the New World, and that apart, they arrived in southern Belize in 1802 long before the Mopan and Kekchi.

The Creoles argue for priority based on the story of the battle of St. George's Cay in 1798.

The Mestizos have taken no back seat to anyone since they have been coming into Belize at least as long ago as the Mayas." – (Ibid.).

Inextricably linked with these issues of identity and ethnicity is race, as well as immigration which has fuelled debate on who should and should not be Belizean. Immigration from Central American countries has also tended to divide Belizeans, pitting black Belizeans – Creoles and Garifunas – against the Maya and Mestizo who usually identify with their brethren from Guatemala, Honduras and other countries in the region entering the Belize:

"During the periodic threats by Guatemala to invade, the Maya leaders of Belize, egged on by overtures to break rank with Belize and support Guatemala refused, and instead declared their unequivocal support for the inviolability of the present Belize borders.

It is difficult to overstate the salience that the Guatemalan dispute makes on Belizean political life not only in relation to the border delimitations but also in regard to the refugee influx and illegal entry of Central Americans into Belize.

With the dramatic influx of 'aliens' into Belize beginning in the early 1980s, this factor came to taint much of Belize's politics and discourse on the issue of ethnic demographic balance. The Creole and Garifuna community was particularly estranged and critical in seeing their comparative numbers eroding.

However, there was another reason for their being critical of the influx stemming from the fact that many of the Central Americans espoused racist attitudes to them referring to the as 'negritos.'[16]

This was experienced first hand on plantations and workplaces in these countries where West Indian Blacks had sought employment.

To be sure, much of this behavior was instigated by 'divide and rule' practices of plantation owners.

Arriving then in Belize, it was not entirely unexpected that many of these 'aliens' received a cold shoulder and worse from Belize's Black population.

The political parties became embroiled in the 'alien' and refugee issue with the United Democratic Party, often identified with the Creole section of the population, openly campaigning against their entry and continued presence.

The People's United party was labeled as sympathetic with Guatemala and the Central Americans, fairly or unfairly, so that in the 1984 elections, the first after independence, when the UDP made 'aliens' its main platform, it successfully evicted the PUP from power.

Again, this happened in 1993 when the British decided to remove most of its troops in Belize, the Central American issue reared its head again resulting in the loss of power of the PUP.

Regardless, under George Price, the PUP leader and Belize's first Prime Minister, his government and party was tarred with the political brush of being pro-Guatemala and Central American.

One educated Creole woman told me bluntly that the present PUP government favored illegal immigration since it provided the votes to win elections.

To be sure, the PUP has showed greater inclination of negotiating with Guatemala and regularizing border relations emphasizing that it was an inescapable part of the geography of Central America.

The UDP on the other hand has recited the mantra of its being Caribbean distancing itself from Guatemala as much as possible.

In all of this, it was also argued that the USA favored the Guatemalan side of the dispute because of the powerful role of the Chiquita banana lobby in the US Congress. Chiquita grows much of its bananas in Guatemala.

The refugee and 'alien' issue has turned on the question of patriotism. I heard it said many times during my trip that Guatemala remains a problem and that not all Belizeans hold Belize with equal loyalty.

I found this position difficult to understand especially in the light that Belizeans prefer to be Belizeans and nobody else with a sense of being unique and different, some of this identity expressed in relation to the Guatemalan 'other.'

Being Belizean makes them more similar to North Americans, a preferred point of reference with which they share the English language.

The migrant influx has also affected labor relations. Trade unions in Belize argue that Central Americans are deliberately recruited as cheap labor so as to marginalise Belizean workers who in turn have developed hostility to the 'alien' presence.

It is argued that it is not true that Belizeans are lazy and refuse to work on the citrus and banana plantations but rather that they were pushed out by cheap labor of the Central Americans.

Finally, the refugee and 'alien' issue had become ethnically criminalised with many Belizeans imputing to the Central Americans not only unhygienic lifestyle but crime and drugs. All of this despite the fact that many refugees and illegal migrants have become permanent residents and citizens, sending their children to English-medium schools and acquiring homes and jobs, with a firm commitment and loyalty to Belize with absolutely no desire to return to their old homes.

In fact, I was reliably told that the children of the migrants have become so anglicized that they risk forgetting their Spanish heritage." – (Ibid.).

But their presence as a people of Spanish heritage in what is considered to be an "Anglo-Saxon" nation, founded by the British and their African slaves, continues to be a contentious issue especially with the ascendancy of the Mestizo as the dominant group in terms of numerical preponderance, and also because of their rapid rise in politics and commerce.

We look at them next.

Mestizo

The biggest ethno-cultural group in Belize today, the Mestizo, is also one of the newest in terms of large population size.

A. product of Spanish ancestry and indigenous roots, the Mestizo became the largest group only recently in the late 1980s and early 1990s when they surpassed the Creole in terms of numbers.

This dramatic shift, in terms of numerical power, from the Creole to the Mestizo has had a profound effect on ethnic relations in Belize, fuelling ethnic consciousness, especially among the Creole, as never before.

This ethnic consciousness revolves around one central issue: who is truly Belizean.

As a group, the Mestizo trace their roots to Mexico. As Belizeans, their history in what is now Belize starts in the 1840s when they first entered the country in large numbers from Mexico, fleeing from the Caste War of Yucatán. And as a racial and ethno-cultural group in the Belizean context, they're very close to Spanish Belizeans who constitute a significant minority.

The Mestizo are also closer to their brethren in Mexico, Guatemala and in other parts of Central America than they are to fellow Belizeans such as the Creole.

That is especially true for those who live in districts close to Guatemala and Mexico. These are Corozal, Orange Walk and Cayo in the northern and northwestern parts of Belize.

This affinity has provided ammunition for some Belizeans who contend that Mestizos are not true Belizeans, a charge that is heard among Creoles probably more than anybody else.

And all the major groups – the Mestizo, the Creole, the Garafuna and the Maya – have resorted to history to buttress their claims.

The Mestizo, the Maya and the Garifuna contend that they have an even more legitimate claim because of their indigenous roots, although not all of them are really native to the region in that sense. The Mestizo are partly Spanish. Therefore they can not claim that they are solely native to Belize or any other part of Central America in a way the Maya are.

The Garifuna also claim ancestral roots as being native to the region because of their Amerindian blood. But that blood is Caribbean, not Central American. The Garifuna also have African blood. In fact, many of them look just like any African in Africa. Therefore they can not claim that they are just "native" to Belize on the basis of ancestry anymore than the Mestizo can. Only the Maya can claim that.

The only group that does not claim native roots, rooted in any part of Central America, is the Creole. Yet it's the most vocal in claiming that it's native to Belize. Its claim is based solely on colonial history which is inextricably linked with the Britain and the Anglo-Saxon tradition.

But regardless of the differences they have, and regardless of the level of ethnic consciousness in all these groups, one fact remains the same. They are all Belizean.

However, that does not in any way diminish their competing claims which are articulated in different ways. As stated in *Perspectives on Las Américas: A Reader in Culture, History, and Representation*:

"The colonists described how they and their slaves had fought together to drive the Spanish away from Belizean waters (at the Battle of St George's Caye in 1798)....Their gallant defense of the settlement, they suggested, had delivered Belize to Britain by right of conquest.

In addition, the 'Baymen' believed they had established a way of life in the settlement which was distinct from and superior to that of the Spanish colonies which surrounded it, organized according to 'British values' of democracy and fairness. They cast Belize as a civilized – Anglo and Anglican – place which they had carved out of former Spanish territory....

153

Thus, from the Baymen's perspective, they had both 'peopled' this territory and fashioned Belize as a distinctive *kind* of place in Central America.

Parts of these claims have devolved today to *creoles*, who are often defined as descendants of the African slaves and 'Baymen' who built the Belizean economy. As Judd (1989) points out, the term *'creole'* itself refers to native status and has been used as a self-identifier in Belize precisely to lay claim to native status." – Matthew C. Gutmann, ed., *Perspectives on Las Américas: A Reader in Culture, History, and Representation*, Wiley-Blackwell; Light Shelfwear edition, 7 February 2003, p. 201).

This interpretation raises fundamental questions about the legitimacy of the claims of other groups who also contend that they are native to Belize and challenges the assumptions of a multicultural society in which all groups are supposed to have equal status.

Other groups have challenged this interpretation of Belizean history precisely because it tends to de-legitimise their status as natives of Belize.

It's a thorny issue especially among the Maya and the Mestizo who claim native ancestry to the region of Central America including what's now Belize although the Mestizo also have Spanish roots.

Yet there is no question that descendants of African slaves played a unique role in the founding of Belize as a nation:

"*Creoles* have legitimized these claims by invoking their participation in the establishment of the forest-based economy which provided the rationale for Belizean existence.

Adopting – sometimes adapting (Hyde 1995) – the legends associated with the Battle of St. George's Caye, some *creoles* have also cast themselves as founders of Belize on the basis of the actions of their forebears – both

154

slave and free – who risked their lives in the battle.

Indeed, self-identified *creoles* played a major role in celebrating and mythologizing the battle as a foundational event in 'Belizean history' one hundred years after it took place (Judd 1989), and a recent article in a local newspaper made oblique reference to the battle two hundred years later to assert priority for Belizeans of African descent: 'Afro-Belizeans built Belize, slaved for it, bled for it, died for it' (Cohen1998: 11).

At the same time, *creole* claims to nativeness also rest heavily on assertions that Belize is more than a geographic territory wrested from the Spanish by their ancestors in 1798. They describe Belize as a culturally unique place in Central America: as a bastion of peace and 'democracy' on a generally violent and undemocratic isthmus (see Fernandez 1989; Medina 1998); as black and Anglo-Caribbean in orientation; as the place in Central America where blacks are least outnumbered and least oppressed (Editorial, *Amandala*, 1991).

Thus, *creole* place making involves the imputation of cultural distinctiveness to Belize and involves claiming a significant role in the creation of the culture which makes Belize unique." (Ibid.).

With this kind of interpretation, the Meztizo, the people who constitute the largest ethno-cultural group in Belize, are seen as foreigners and even as invaders who simply flocked into Belize from neighbouring countries to uproot and displace the native Creoles.

The big influx of Mestizos into Belize since the 1980s has definitely changed the ethnic balance in the country and has tipped scales in their favour in terms of numbers. How this is going to affect the country and determine the course of events in that multicultural society, including allocation of jobs and resources, is a matter for speculation.

But with Creoles being in control of important sectors

in the country, conflict is bound to occur since the Mestizo are now seen as a threat to the Creole community.

It's also highly probable that the Creole will form a strong alliance with the Garifuna who, like the Creole, claim native status in Belize and have African ancestry which equally legitimises their claim as founders of Belize even though their history of slavery is traced to the Caribbean:

"The Garifuna, clearly immigrants, also lay claim to 'native status,' but they use different kinds of arguments to buttress their claims.

Although they have obtained national recognition for Settlement Day, a holiday which celebrates the early 19th-century arrival of Garifuna in Belize (Macklin 1986), their assertion of 'native' status is based more on their embrace of a dual ancestry which includes African and Carib forebears.

Their Carib ancestry makes them *indigenous to the Caribbean*. Indeed, Belizean Garifuna belong to Caribbean Organization of Indigenous Peoples, which also includes the Caribs of St. Vincent (from where the Garifuna were expelled by the British).

Forcibly deported by the British from their home in the eastern Caribbean to the shores of Central America, they claim nativity in Belize in terms of the larger Caribbean region to which they – and Belize – belong.

In asserting native 'status' for themselves, they also emphasize their non-western (Arawakan) language and cultural practices (Kerns 1983; Gonzalez 1986, 1988). Further, although most Garifuna have embraced the arguments presented by anthropologists and historians that the Africans incorporated into Carib society were slaves who escaped, were shipwrecked, or were carried away during Carib raids on colonial settlements (Gonzalez 1988; Cayetano n.d..), some Garifuna have drawn upon Van Sertima's (1976) argument *They Came Before Columbus* to extend the arrival of their African ancestors in the Americas further into antiquity (Kirby,1997)." (Ibid., pp. 201 - 202).

That is an Afrocentric myth which has been challenged even by Africans themselves including myself.

The tendency by many Afrocentric scholars to re-write history and distort facts to promote their political agenda is a great disservice to scholarship and to Africa.

It's also a disservice to the people of African descent in the diaspora. It's mis-education of the black race by blacks themselves. Fortunately, not all of us subscribe to these Afrocentric myths.

The Garifuna can legitimately claim native status in Belize on the basis of how long they have been there probably more than anything else; and on the basis of native ancestry in a larger Caribbean context which culturally includes Belize as a former British colony that had African slaves just like all he other Anglophone countries in the region.

The claims by the Creoles and the Garifuna pose the biggest challenge to counter-claims by the Mestizo. Unlike the Creole and the Garifuna, the Mestizo are relatively new immigrants in Belize although the first ones arrived there in the 1840s. But most of them arrived later, especially in the 1980s.

The numerical superiority of the Mestizo is also seen as a threat not only to the Creole but also to the Garifuna. The Mestizo are also seen as natural allies of the Maya because of the indigenous roots they share just as the Creole share African roots with the Garifuna, also making them natural allies.

But although the Mestizo also claim native status, they have not articulated their claim in a consistent and forceful manner the way the Creole, and to a smaller extent, the Garifuna have; a point underscored in a work edited by Matthew C. Gutmann, *Perspectives on Las Américas: A*

"*Mestizos* also at times make claims to 'native' status, though they have not done so collectively. In fact, *mestizos* are the least organized of the major ethnic categories in Belize.

The implication of 'mixture' associated with the *mestizo* label imputes 'native' ancestry at some point in the past. (And) while relations between *mestizo* and Maya in Belize have been hierarchically structured, the differences and hierarchical ordering at present appear to be less extreme in Belize than in neighboring countries.

Recent decades have seen a great deal of boundary crossing in northern Belize as economic opportunities in commercial agriculture opened up....Many families shifted from Yucatec Maya to *mestizo* identities (Brockmann, 1977, 1985; Birdwell-Pheasant 1985; Henderson 1990; Wilk 1996).

Wilk and Chapin's designation of this population as 'Spanish-speaking *mestizos* mostly of Maya ancestry' reflects these shifts and the ambiguity they have produced (Wilk and Chapin, 1990: 7).

Belizean-born *mestizos* generally make claims to nativeness in response to challenges by *creoles* or Garifuna, who often confound them with the Central American immigrants who arrived in Belize in 1980s." (Ibid., p. 202)

Sometimes, these competing claims to native status have led to public exchanges. They have also raised the level of racial and cultural consciousness and pride in Central American heritage one does not always hear from the Mestizo especially when it relates to the Maya whom they consider to be beneath them.

The result has been some kind of closing of ranks between the Mestizo and the Maya against a common problem: assertion of cultural and historical "supremacy" by the Creole as the only native Belizeans:

"Notwithstanding the hierarchical ordering of *mestizo* and Maya categories, when challenged like this individual *mestizos* sometimes invoke their imputed Mayan ancestry to assert the legitimacy of their presence in Belize and the depth of their 'roots' there.

For example, at a soccer match I attended in 1990, which pitted a Belizean team against a team from Guatemala, I was seated near a group of *mestizo* Belizeans, who were cheering for the Belizean team. During the second half of the match, with the Belizean team trailing, an Afro-Brazilian man – rather drunk – stopped in front of the bleachers and turned to shout at the *mestizo* fans, 'Aliens! Go back where you came from!'

One of the *mestizo* women shouted back, 'I'm as Belizean as you are! We're from Benque! If you ever came out to Benque you would see that there are no blacks there, but it's still Belize, and we are Belizeans!'

Benque is a town near the border with Guatemala, whose population is largely classified as *mestizo* (though it was earlier known as a Maya community (Jones 1977).

Her assertion that 'there are no blacks there, but it's still Belize,' indicated her understanding of the man's logic: blacks can be assumed to be Belizeans; others cannot (see Medina 1997). But she challenged his assumption by arguing that *mestizos* can be 'as Belizean as' he is.

'All of you just crossed the river!' the man retorted, asserting that the woman and her companions were Guatemalans who had recently crossed the border illegally, and that their presence in Belize was therefore illegitimate.

Growing angry, the *mestizo* woman asserted the legitimacy of her presence in Belize on the basis of the 'native' origins implied by the *mestizo* label. She answered, 'My people were in Belize long before the white man brought you as a slave!'

159

Her reply reversed their identities, casting herself as the 'native' and her adversary as the immigrant." (Ibid.).

The Mestizo also claim native status in a much larger context in the sense that the region that is now Central America, which includes Belize, belonged to their ancestors long before the white man came; while black Belizeans are no more than immigrants who were taken there by the white man as slaves from their ancestral homeland: Africa.

Even Belizean immigrants from other parts of Central America who were not even born in Belize claim indigenous status which black Belizeans don't have. One of the largest groups of immigrants who came from other parts of Central America are Guatelamans.

Although of Guatemalan origin, they claim they are just as Belizean because Belize is part of an entire region which belongs to the indigenous people of whom they are in integral part; a position forcefully articulated by one Guatemalan who had a fiery exchange with a black Belizean who questioned the legitimacy of Guatemalan presence in Belize. According to an account in a study of Central America, *Perspectives on Las Américas: A Reader in Culture, History, and Representation*:

"Even immigrants from Guatemala who see themselves as *ladino* – a label best defined as the *opposite* of 'Indian' – sometimes claim indigenous heritage when their presence in Belize is challenged by Belizeans. For example, a Guatemalan immigrant, who had been working in Belize for years, recounted this story of a confrontation he experienced as he was returning by bus from a visit to Guatemala.

An Afro-Brazilian man seated behind him on the bus asked him what he was doing 'in a black country.' The Guatemalan asserted on behalf of himself and a Guatemalan travelling companion, 'We are Indians; we are

160

from here. I am on my continent! The white people brought you here as a slave, but this continent is ours.'

These claims to nativeness by both Belizean-born and immigrant *mestizos* locate themselves in a region larger than Belize itself; indeed, the last example claims a continental indigenousness.

Further, *mestizos* tend not to refer to a particular indigenous identity, but rather to a *generic* one: 'Indian.' Its genericness suggests a great time depth for the 'mixture' in one's ancestry, such that specifics are no lonGer known – perhaps making them 'less' Indian while still allowing them to claim that ancestry." (Ibid., pp. 202 – 203).

Mestizos do, indeed, have native roots on the basis of their Maya ancestry even though they're also partly white. Their European ancestors, the Spanish conquistadors, even enslaved the Maya, the ancestors of the Mestizo today.

It's also true that they are Belizean just like anybody else who is a citizen of Belize even without native status. And they are now the largest ethnic group in Belize.

But, in spite of their numerical superiority, the Mestizo are a cultural minority in Belize because they live in a country whose dominant culture is Kriol – or Creole – derived from the Anglo-Saxon tradition as a former British colony.

They also live in a country whose main language is English, not Spanish which would be more natural for them as a people of Spanish ancestry even if only partly so. It's even more frustrating to them when they see that Belize is in a region that is predominantly Spanish in terms of language and culture – with the exception of Belize itself.

In fact, most of them speak Spanish as their first language. And most of them speak Spanish at home.

But they also know that they must learn English, the language of their "cultural superiors" – the Creole – because that's the main language used in school, at work, in government offices, in business and in other areas of national life.

They know that in order for them to prosper, get jobs and be able to go to school all they way to university, they must learn English.

So, from a cultural and linguistic point of view, the Mestizo are subordinate to the Creole. And that will continue to be the case as long as the main cultural influence in the country is Kriol, and as long as the national language of Belize continues to be English, as it most likely will be.

But the Mestizo are also some of the best educated people in Belize. They are also some of the most successful in the economic arena.

Many other Belizeans resent that. They see the Mestizo – legal or not – as aliens who have flocked into the country from Guatemala, Mexico, Honduras and other parts of Central America to take jobs and everything else that belongs to "native" Belizeans. It makes no difference even if some of the Mestizo they complain about were born in Belize. To some Belizeans, they're still "foreigners."

This resentment is more widespread among black Belizeans, or Creoles, who see Mestizos as a real threat to their wellbeing. They have seen them seize opportunities – in employment, education, politics and other areas of national life – which before had been enjoyed by black Belizeans. They have also seen them replace black Belizeans as the largest ethnic group in the country.

And the change seems to be permanent, further fuelling resentment against the Mestizo, a term that also has a much broader definition in the Belizean context than it does elsewhere in Latin America. As Professor Irma McClaurin states in her book *Women of Belize: Gender and Change in Central America*:

"Whereas in the general context of Latin America, 'Mestizo' refers to people of Spanish and Amerindian culture, in Belize it is a generic designation for anyone who adheres to Spanish language and culture. Thus in Belize, regardless of national origin, Argentineans, Costa Ricans, Spaniards, and Puerto Ricans all become homogenized as 'Mestizo,' sometimes referred to derisively by mostly Creole Belizeans as 'Spanish.'

Even Mestizos in Belize participate in this ritual of communality, and it is this aspect of nondistinction that has made it easy for refugees from neighboring countries to blend in. If these newcomers master the Creole language, they are indistinguishable from native-born Mestizos, a fact that has created some problems for the latter.

Creoles, as a result of their large numbers during the earliest part of the country's formation, have largely shaped Belizean culture. Although, according to the 1991 census, they represent only 29.6 percent of the population as compared with 39.7 percent in 1980, their language is the everyday medium of communication, and cultural preferences for reggae and soca music permeate the airways more than any other musical form.

At one time Creoles dominated most of the important occupations, especially in the civil service arena. Today, though they remain part of Belize's cultural mosaic, their influence is diminishing, largely due to attrition via emigration to the United States.

Their shrinking numbers and the increased presence of other groups who adhere to Spanish in language and culture has created a crisis of identity for Creole Belizeans." – (Irma McClaurin, *Women of Belize: Gender and Change in Central America*, Newark, New Jersey: Rutgers University, 1 August 1996, p. 32).

This identity crisis goes to the heart of the problem the Creole community faces in Belize: As the people who laid the foundation of what became the nation of Belize, do they really have a place in the country they founded if they are overwhelmed by other groups, especially Mestizos most of whom have entered the country in massive numbers in recent years? Are they still going to remain powerful? Are they going to lose their identity and culture? As Professor McClaurin goes on to state:

"Creoles now engage in debates over whether they have a culture, over whether Creole is an 'authentic' language or just a denigrated form of English.

Notwithstanding those who might wish to disparage it, Creole culture and identity are key aspects of Belize's general national culture, its food, language, and ambiance.

Having fallen from a position of ethnic ascendancy, Creoles now find themselves increasingly at the lower end of privilege, and new tensions and antagonisms increasingly surface as they perceive newcomers as encroachers.

Some Creoles hold the large influx of Central American refugees responsible for their current lowered socioeconomic position. They feel the new immigrants do not truly wish to become Belizean, but only want to take advantage of resources such as land, government-subsidized education, and other social services unavailable in their countries of origin – a view shared by other Belizean ethnic groups as well." – (Ibid.).

In addition to being a threat to their socioeconomic position, Creoles see another danger posed by the new comers. The influx of these immigrants is also seen as a form of cultural invasion which threatens to erode and may be even eventually replace Creole culture if unchecked.

The introduction of new lifestyles by the immigrants in Belize may add to the multicultural mix but it also undermines established ways. And when a new culture is introduced, new values are also propagated in society, including violence as a way of life.

The people who come from neighbouring countries such as Guatemala are seen as a violent people who are a product of societies where violence is a way of life. That is in sharp contrast with life in Belize where, although not free from violence, the people live in relative harmony in spite of the tensions within.

This feeling and perception is especially strong among the Creoles or black Belizeans.

But it's not confined to Central American immigrants. It's also directed against other groups whom the Creole see as a threat to them, even if not as threatening as the Mestizo.

Still, the perceived violence of the new comers from Guatemala and other parts of Central America, and the danger posed by other immigrants, especially Asians, to the wellbeing of black Belizeans provide a deadly combination which can be very harmful to inter-ethnic relations between black Belizeans and other groups. As Professor McClaurin states:

"Moreover, they (Creoles) feel these new comers bring with them a lifestyle premised on violence.

I have been warned by Creole friends to travel with caution. A Belizean will rob you, I am told, but the – Central American – refugees will rob you and kill you. They have grown accustomed to violence because of the conflict in their countries, or so some Belizeans believe.

Whether fact or fiction, the belief shapes people's attitudes, creates stereotypes, guides behavior, and stretches taut the growing band of tension among ethnic groups today.

Nowhere is this tension more noticeable than in social relations between Creoles and Asians – Chinese and newly arrived East Indians.

Unlike Mestizos, who are concentrated in their own districts, Asians now reside in close proximity in Belize City to Creoles, who formerly made up the dominant segment of the urban population.

The dislike between Asians and Creoles appears to be mutual, and the irrefutable divide is symbolized by the iron bars that grace many Chinese businesses in Belize City.

The bars, while an obvious defense against crime, which is sometimes ethnically based, also signal an unspoken desire by many Chinese to remain aloof and separate from the rest of the Belizean society. In addition, the Chinese style of interaction seems to most local Belizeans to be rude and intolerant.

The tensions between East Indians and Creoles seem less strained in comparison. However, new East Indians living in the city remain fairly endogamous, speak their own language, and generally interact very little with Creoles outside of the merchant-customer dyad.

Finally, many Belizeans, especially Creoles, express anger at the commercial success of Asians who, while forming a very small portion of the population, dominate the retail market. Their family-oriented mode of operating excludes Belizeans who seek employment, for jobs are given to relatives, children and spouses.

Further, urban Creole entrepreneurs not only lack the initial capital but appear more individualistic in their orientation, and so do not subscribe to the ethnic solidarity that enables East Indian merchants to pool resources to purchase stock and sometimes share facilities." – (Ibid., pp. 32 – 33).

The tensions also assume cultural and linguistic dimensions in a society that is predominantly Creole in terms of culture.

The refusal by many new immigrants to learn Kriol, the country's main language, and adopt Creole culture is a source of tension between these new comers and the Creole. The Creole see them as foreigners who have come into their country. Yet they refuse to become true

166

Belizeans.

Their refusal to learn Kriol and embrace Creole culture may also undermine the nation's social fabric which is based on Creole culture, if the trend continues.

It's also clear that Creole culture has functioned well as a glue, helping to hold the nation together. Without a common national culture, the different ethno-cultural groups which collectively constitute Belize as a nation would not have been able to live in harmony as much as they do now.

The unwillingness by some immigrants to learn the Kriol language has also introduced a new element in the cultural mix that did not exist before on such a scale. And it has exacerbated ethnic tensions:

"Few of the newcomers to Belize bother to learn the Creole language.

The failure to speak Creole introduces into what has traditionally seemed an ideal ethnic complex a new element of intercultural tensions and linguistic misunderstanding, especially with those populations that are non-Spanish speaking – most Creoles have some familiarity with Spanish, and those living in the northern, southern, or western districts possess a certain degree of proficiency.

Although other ethnic groups in the country do not as a general rule adhere rigidly to endogamy – though intermarriages between Creoles and Garifuna seem rarer than between Creoles and Mestizos or Maya, or between Creoles and East Indians – the newer Asian immigrants tend to be more strict in their practices, marrying primarily within their group or importing spouses for themselves and their children.

All of this contributes to a proliferation of ethnic stereotypes, exacerbates feelings of economic exclusion on the part of Creoles, and threatens to bring closer to the surface whatever ethnic tensions may lie hidden in the recesses of Belize's past." – (Ibid., p. 33).

Right now, Mestizos are the biggest threat to Creoles who remain the dominant group in Belize in terms of culture. Theirs is the majority culture embraced by almost all Belizeans even if grudgingly so.

Yet, in spite of the success among Mestizos in terms of education and in other areas, there are many of them who are not as educated as the Creoles are, thus reinforcing their subordinate status as a cultural minority in a country whose dominant culture is Creole. And that translates into lower social and economic status for uneducated Mestizos or those who don't have much education since they can not compete with the Creole on the basis of merit in many areas of employment and upward mobility.

However, the Mestizo are a major force in politics in Belize. They're also prominent in business. Their status in society is also reinforced by the fact that they look white because of their Spanish ancestry. In fact, many of them have very little native – Amerindian – blood and are really white.

They're called Spanish in Belize and many Belizeans assume they come from other parts of Spanish-speaking Central America. And Belizeans already hostile towards Spanish immigrants from the other countries in the region also direct their anger towards the Mestizos in spite of the fact that they're fellow Belizeans born and brought up in Belize.

The dramatic increase in the Mestizo population in Belize has also fuelled competition with black Belizeans some of which assumes racial dimensions. Not all Mestizos surpass blacks. But even those who fail still think they are better than blacks.

Some of them seek solace in their perceived superiority to blacks who are seen by many people in other races to be members of an inferior race.

Even in the black community itself, there is a tendency

to value "white" colour. It's a belief that is prevalent even among some of the most educated dark-skinned Creoles in Belize. As Professor Ralph Premdas states in his study, "Belize: Identity and Ethnicity in a Multi-Ethnic State":

"In a multi-ethnic, multi-lingual and multi-racial setting such as in Belize City, it is reasonable to inquire into the problem of communal coexistence and tolerance. I gather that it is not an issue, at least not overly expressed but as one person said to me 'hush hush.'

One fascinating observation that I made regarding the migrant women was that a few were mates of Creoles. Racial mixing was quite unconcealed and prevalent in Belize. No one neither looked nor cared. It seemed that Belize was a veritable melting pot of races and ethnicities, at least on the surface.

However, one local observer said to me that the incidence of Creole liaisons with the Central American refugees allowed for a 'whitening' via offspring towards acquiring higher social status.

In the insular Caribbean, a colour-class stratification continues to prevail privileging degrees of whiteness even after most of these countries became independent accompanied with the rise to power and position of Creoles.

In Belize, colour evidently continues to matter, especially in the Creole community. One famous editor of a newspaper referred to this phenomenon as 'colourism.'"
– Ralph R. Premdas, "Belize: Identity and Ethnicity in a Multi-Ethnic State," a paper presented at the Belize Country Conference, University of West Indies, Cave Hill, Barbados, 21 – 24 November 2001).

But this does not change the fact that many dark-skinned Creoles are doing better than many Mestizos in many areas of life.

The two groups are locked in competition and in many

ways resent each other, although open resentment against other groups is not a widespread phenomenon in Belize as it is in some countries. But even if it's latent, it's still just as destructive, for example, in terms of opportunities denied simply because you "don't belong."

It's not uncommon for members of the same group, any group, to help each other in areas of employment and so on while ignoring or excluding those who don't belong to their group. It's even worse when some groups are locked in competition or are hostile towards each other as is the case with black Belizeans and Mestizos; although their relationship is better described as one of competition rather than outright hostility.

But there are times when some members of an even major group such as the Creole have been openly hostile towards smaller groups whom they also consider to be a threat to them. The attitude of some black Belizeans towards the Chinese clearly demonstrate that.

Although the Chinese are not really new in Belize, they're still seen as "foreigners" even if the people who don't want them there know that the first Chinese arrived in Belize – in what was then British Honduras – in the 1860s. Many others arrived much later, of course, but that makes no difference to some Belizeans who think and believe that Belize belongs only to them. All "foreigners," whether they're new immigrants or not, are "foreigners," and not "true" Belizeans.

Probably more than any other group in Belize, with the possible exception of East Indians, the Chinese have become the most visible minority group which has been targeted by some black Belizeans for exclusion from Belizean society, a problem compounded by the Chinese themselves many of whom don't want to be fully integrated into society, especially with the black Belizeans. As Professor Premdas stated in his report which he wrote after his study tour of Belize in 2001:

"Early in my visit, I looked around for restaurants and small stores to procure some groceries. It was very startling to discover that a very large number of these small shops found practically everywhere in Belize City and in many parts of the country were owned and operated by Chinese who had little command of English.

I knew that some Chinese had come to Belize round about 1865 as indentured laborers. It was clear that these Chinese storeowners were not descended from that early community.

In Belize, while many of the old Chinese families have migrated and left, a number have remained and currently control several prominent businesses. Several have also intermarried with other ethnic groups and generally they are Belizean as anyone could be.

The Chinese population in Belize however is quite varied with many arriving in separate waves in the 1960s, 1980s and 1990s, with those arriving in the 1960s relatively integrated in the social fabric and quite different from recent arrivals who speak very little if any English.

Many of the recent arrivals have come as economic residents taking advantage of a government policy, rescinded in 2002, that offered Belize citizenship to foreigners with substantial capital for investment.

It was clear that the Chinese shops were family affairs and that nearly all of the Chinese who I have encountered had only the barest of links to the rest of the Belizean population. In Belize City, the Chinese have also opened a handful of restaurants.

Asking Belizeans about the new Chinese residents in their midst, I found out that there was some resentment in that the Chinese seemed to have gained control of the small scale stores, displacing many Belizeans. None of this was expressed either strongly or openly.

Many of the robberies in Belize are directed against Chinese storeowners, allegedly committed by Creole gangs. It is a sore area stirring some inter-ethnic malaise.

Another aspect of the Chinese presence in Belize relates to the illegal sale of passports. Many recent arrivals, it was alleged, had acquired passports before ever setting foot in Belize, suggesting complicity between immigration officers and passport buyers....

Overall then Belize City was marked by ethnic diversity with three recent immigrant groups: the 'alien' Central American migrants, the Chinese entrepreneurs, and the Indian and Middle Eastern merchant groups adding to the melange but still not challenging the dominant numbers of Creoles in the city.

I saw no resident Whites from the old English plantocracy but saw many Whites who were tourists." – (Ibid.).

Although Black Belizeans feel threatened by the Mestizos and even by the Chinese and other smaller groups of immigrants engaged in commerce, they remain a dominant force in Belize. And they're even further ahead of the Maya who are on the lowest rung of the social and economic ladder as the most disadvantaged group in Belize.

We look at the Maya next.

Maya

There is a paradoxical situation in Belize. The most indigenous people are the least developed group in the country. They're the poorest and most powerless. They're also the least educated.

These people are the Maya.

They were the first to inhabit the region that is now Central America, including Belize. They were also the first to be conquered. When Europeans first arrived, they found the Maya, a people with an advanced civilisation.

They fought hard but they lost. They did not have

172

advanced weapons to be able to defeat their invaders. That is the technological theory of imperialism, validated in the Mayan context with devastating consequences as much as it was in other parts of the world, including Africa, which were conquered by Europeans.

And when Europeans, the British in particular, established an outpost of Western civilisation in the area that came to be known as British Honduras, which is now Belize, the Maya remained a subjugated people. Even slaves brought from Africa eventually emerged to become some of the most powerful people in Belize, while the indigenous people, the Maya, remained at the bottom.

Today, the Maya constitute a significant part of Belize's population, bigger than other groups such as the Chinese and East Indians, yet far less successful.

They live in different parts of the country but mostly in the west and northwest (Cayo and Orange Walk districts, respectively), and in the south (Toledo District), their strongholds.

And they belong to different groups although they're united by a common heritage collectively known as Maya, in spite of the differences within. And in relation to other groups which are not Maya, for example the Creole and Asian immigrants, the distinction is clear.

They are the true natives of the land. All the others are immigrants even if they claim native status, as descendants of African slaves do, contending that they're the true founding fathers of Belize as a nation since they formed the backbone of the economy which led to the establishment of British Honduras as a colony which eventually became the independent nation of Belize.

While it's true that African slaves and their descendants laid the economic foundation of what came to be known as Belize, and the British colony would not have survived without the labour from these African slaves; it's equally true that the original inhabitants of the land where the nation of Belize was established were the Maya. Without their land, there would be no Belize today. And, of course, without the labour of African slaves, there would be no Belize today, either.

Therefore both have legitimate claims to native status in Belize although from different perspectives, neither of which is better or more legitimate than the other.

Although their claim to indigenous status may carry more weight in terms of history as the original owners of the land – and not as the founders of the nation (blacks claim and deserve that more than anybody else) – they have not been able to articulate their demands effectively as true citizens of Belize because of their weakness.

There is no better proof for that than their desperately poor condition when compared with other ethnic groups in the country. Not only are they the poorest; they are the most neglected.

But although they have not been as vocal as the Creole and other groups in their claims, they have nevertheless taken a strong position on their status in the context of Belize as a multi-racial and multi-cultural society. When Professor Ralph Premdas made a study tour of Belize in April 2001, he came up with these observations about the Maya and their claims which were disputed by other groups just as strongly:

"It was in Toledo that the Mayas were claiming a Maya Homeland of some half a million acres.

My entry into Toledo signaled meeting the largest concentration of peoples of Mayan extraction in Belize. Southwest Belize and the Mayan Mountains are the home of such large Mayan settlements as San Antonio.

I was intrigued with this Mayan category since none of the countries of the Caribbean possessed any such grouping; Belize did and for someone coming from the insular Caribbean based in Trinidad, the idea of a Mayan had the exotic aura of novelty.

To be sure, before arriving in Belize, I had read about

some very large new archaeological digs of ancient Mayan settlements in Belize, and that apart, I have read a fair amount of materials about the Mayas in Central America. However, my prior knowledge of the Mayas in Belize was practically zero.

I was equally unprepared for the contestations that I would encounter regarding the Mayas and their identity and claims in Belize.

It was in Toledo that these issues were in turmoil focused around the argument that the Mayas of the Toledo District were indigenous to that part of Belize. The Maya Cultural Council of Toledo based in PG, claimed indigenous status of the Mayas as a means of justifying ownership of a vast area that they wanted to be officially declared a 'Maya Homeland.'

The other communities of Creoles, Garifuna, and East Indians in the district challenged this view arguing that Belize was a country of immigrants and that the Mayas of the Toledo district were relatively recent arrivals like everyone else in the area and consequently the claim of a 'Mayan Homeland' was not justified.

The school books used throughout Belize recite a clear narrative that conceded that there were Mayan settlements in Belize prior to the arrival of the British woodcutters in the early seventeenth century, but proceed to point out that the present day Mayans in Belize were not descended from this original community of Mayas. Rather, they were recent arrivals and in some cases arriving later than the Creoles and Garifuna.

The Mayas in Belize are classified in these school textbooks as belonging to three groupings:

The Yucatec, who now live predominantly in Corozal and Orange Walk Districts, originated in the 19th century from the Yucatan as a result of the dislocations caused by the Caste Wars. Today, they have adapted to Spanish and English cultural practices and gave up much of their traditional customs and rituals.

175

The Mopan, who today are found mainly in San Antonio in Toledo District and in a number of Villages in Cayo District, came to Belize in 1876 running away from taxation and forced labor in Peten.

The Kekchi, who today live in southeast lowland river areas of Toledo, came to Belize in the 1870s fleeing from plantation enslavement in Verapaz, Guatemala.

Among the Mopan and Kekchi of Toledo, this history is sharply challenged. They both claim ancestry of the Mayas and thus are entitled to the status of the 'first' inhabitants of Belize with collateral entitlements.

In Toledo, the Mopan and Kekchi dwell on small parcels of reserve land given to them by the state but they complain that it is very inadequate to sustain their traditional life as slash and burn milpa farmers.

It was in 1980 when the Mopan of Toledo first registered their claim for a Mayan Homeland encompassing some half a million acres. The request was not conceded but it has triggered a fierce debate among the various ethnocultural communities in Toledo about the authenticity of the 'nativeness' of the Mayans in the areas that they claim.

Interestingly, since history is treated as an important tool in constructing a group's identity and registering its claims and complaints, all the communities in Belize have evolved their own historical narrative with each claiming the status of being native and indigenous." – (Ibid.)

Still, it's obvious that there were no Africans in Belize or anywhere else in Central America before Europeans went there and conquered the indigenous people; which means there were no Creoles and no Garifunas.

Also, there were no Mestizos since they're a product of intermarriage and other relationships between the indigenes and their Spanish conquerors. And that leaves the Maya alone as the original owners of the land, until they lost it when settlers from Spain, and in the case of

Belize from Britain, took it by force.

But their claims to indigenous status in Belize are also contested on the basis of the nation's history, how the country evolved to be what it is today; not merely on the basis of who owned the land first, or who was "here first." As stated in the work edited by Matthew C. Gutmann, *Perspectives on Las Américas: A Reader in Culture, History, and Representation*:

"Although the Mopan and Kekchi can claim more specific identities, the history of 19th-century immigration from Guatemala has confounded their efforts to claim native identity in Belize *as* Mopan and Kekchi.

If historical accounts of the early colonial period are disputed, and names applied to fluid socio-political groupings are contested, Belizean textbooks have been clear in their references to the 19th-century immigration of Mopan and Kekchi from Guatemala. Thus Mopan and Kekchi are widely understood to be immigrants to Belize like everyone else....

Some ethnographers and historians have argued for a persistent Mopan presence in western Belize (Shoman 1994; Stone 1994), and others cite evidence of a continual indigenous presence in southern Belize, in spite of the Spanish removal of much of the population (Wilk, 1997, n.d.).

Further, Thompson has suggested that the Manche Chols, who the Spanish forcibly removed from southern Belize, were absorbed by the Kekchi, such that Kekchi migration to southern Belize represents a *return* (Thompson 1988: 6).

However, given the fact of Mopan and Kekchi immigration in the late 1800s, their most persuasive claims to 'native' status may be based on an identification as Maya rather than as Mopan or Kektchi.

'Indian' and 'Maya' labels and identities emerged during the 1960s and 1970s, as road construction in southern

177

Belize led to intensified interactions with other categories of Belizeans (Gregory 1984; Howard 1975).

Embracing a broad 'Indian' or 'Maya' label rather than narrower Mopan or Kekchi identities, Mopan and Kekchi leaders formed the Toledo Maya Cultural Council in 1978. The TMCC claims ancestry from the ancient Maya, to whose presence in Belizean territory 'Mayan ruins' attest."
– (Matthew C. Gutmann, *Perspectives on Las Américas: A Reader in Culture, History, and Representation*, op.cit., p. 203).

This broader claim, and rooted in ancient history, legitimises claims to native status in Belize – by Amerindian groups which collectively constitute the Maya – which may not have been justified on the basis of recent history of the establishment of the Belizean nation which did not exist before the coming of the British who also brought African slaves to help create this nation.

The argument based on ancient history of the Mayan empire also implies that the indigenous people not only owned the land for thousands of years; they still owned it even after they were expelled by the white settlers and have simply reclaimed it when they returned there even if it's only in recent years:

"The TMCC argues that Maya migration into Toledo in the 1800s involved 'returning to our ancestral lands....Most of the Ke'kchi and Mopan Maya came in groups from neighboring Guatemala to find their roots here in Belize' (TMCC and TAA 1997: 9). They ask,

How can we, Mayas, be considered immigrants? We are the original inhabitants of Toledo Belize who know no boundaries....

The Mayas of Toledo are the direct descendants of the ancient Mayas whose civilization reached its peak around A.D. 900. The continuous use of the Maya temples for religious purposes is testimony to their connection with the past (TMCC and TAA 1997: 2 – 3).

As Maya, they can more convincingly claim a

continual presence in Belizean territory. Thus, Mayan identity may confer indigenous status upon its holder in a way which Kekchi or Mopan identity cannot.

Mopan and Kekchi claims to 'native' status made as Mayas or Indians resonate strongly beyond Belize; the TMCC has found support in international organizations which represent or work on behalf of indigenous peoples....

Indeed, a report produced for the Toledo Maya Cultural Council by the Indian Law Resource Center in the U.S., explicitly defines Mopan and Kekchi as Maya and counters arguments which label them as immigrants to Belize:

[I]t would be a mistake to make too much of the Spanish efforts to expel the Maya.

The fact that some Maya may have been removed against their will across what was then an imaginary border, only to return 150 years later, does not mean that the Maya abandoned their homeland or relinquished their aboriginal rights to Toledo District.

The aboriginal territories of the Maya encompassed southern Belize and the area across the border in Guatemala. From the Maya point of view, their land was a single territory that could not be divided by an artificial border drawn by non-Indian colonial powers (Berkey 1994: 3 – 4)." (Ibid. pp. 203 - 204).

In all these claims to native status by various groups in Belize, one argument stands out for its striking parallels to imperial logic in the context of Africa. And that is the claim to native status by the Creoles. As one black Belizean stated in the country's largest newspaper:

"The Afro-Belizeans built Belize, slaved for it, bled for it, died for it." – (ibid., p. 205).

While all that is true, the argument they make is not very much different from what the British settlers in Rhodesia, now Zimbabwe, used – except that they didn't slave for it but instead it was the Africans who slaved for it under their white masters.

It's also the same argument the white minorities used in South Africa to justify their right to be the owners of the land on the basis that they were the founders of the nation. As South African Prime Minister Hendrik Verwoerd stated in the South African parliament on 3 February 1960: "We are the people who brought civilisation to Africa."

He was responding to what British Prime Minister Harold MacMillan said in the same parliament and on the same day: "The wind of change is blowing through this continent, and whether we like it or not, this growth of national consciousness is a political fact."

Years later, the wind of change blew across Rhodesia and South Africa, the citadel of white supremacy on the continent, and brought about fundamental change.

It's true that what was then the British colony of Rhodesia, now Zimbabwe, did not exist before the coming of Europeans; nor did the country of South Africa. But that does not mean that the indigenous people in those countries did not have legitimate claims to native status on the land – hence ownership of the land – where these two countries were founded by the colonial rulers.

And it does not mean that the settlers from Europe and immigrants from other parts of the world who live in those countries are mere guests who have no rights black Zimbabweans and black South Africans are bound to respect.

Claims to native status in a multi-racial and multicultural society challenge the assumptions of a democratic nation built on the premise that individual rights take precedence over groups rights. And when the two clash, the former must prevail.

And any continuation of such demands by different groups, each claiming special rights and privileges or special status, is bound to destroy the very foundation upon which a democratic society is founded.

Belize has not reached that point. And it may not go

that far. But there must be ways to balance the interests of the nation and the interests of various ethno-cultural groups which collectively constitute the nation in order for everybody, individuals as well as groups, to have equal rights and status in a multicultural society.

It is a multicultural perspective. And there seems to be no other way to look at the complex realities of life in a nation like Belize which is a product of many races, cultures and ethnic groups from different parts of the world.

Part Three:

Life in Belize

LIFE in Belize is not very much different from life in other parts of the developing world.

Belize is an integral part of the Third World. It's not a developed country like the United States and Canada, two of the most developed countries in the Western Hemisphere; nor is it developed like Barbados or Argentina.

Barbados is the most developed country in the Caribbean. In fact, it's one of the three most developed countries in the Western Hemisphere after the United States and Canada.

And Argentina is the most developed country in Latin America.

Belize is nowhere close to that.

Even its urban centres are not very developed. They are not even cities but towns. They all have small populations and poor infrastructure. And that includes Belize City, the largest urban centre in the country even though it's called a city. And almost all of them are typical Third World urban centres.

But they also have bright spots as almost all towns and cities in Third World countries do.

Yet life even in these few urban centres in Belize is not comparable to life in the United States or in other parts of the industrialised world except in a few cases.

The establishment of towns or urban centres in Belize has followed a historical pattern determined by economics probably more than anything else.

In many cases, they are a product of communities established along waterways – on the coast and on river banks – to facilitate transport of logwood and mahogany, the backbone of the economy when the colony was founded in the 1600s.

The same pattern still exists today for almost all the towns in Belize. Few are built away from rivers and the coast.

Inextricably linked with its past as a country founded on the forestry industry – mainly timber – is the way houses are built in Belize. Houses are built mainly of wood. It was easy to find timber to build houses when the lumber business was booming. Many of those houses still stand today.

The use of wood to build houses has now become an integral part of national culture because of this historical pattern. In many cases, it was the preferred building material, especially before 1960.

But forces of nature helped to change this pattern. Wooden houses were destroyed by hurricanes, forcing many people to start using ferro-concrete to build houses which had a better chance of withstanding some of the damage caused by furious storms and hurricanes.

Still, Belize is a tropical paradise, and a gateway to Central America, but with remarkable contrasts in the way different groups of people live.

In his book *Living Abroad in Belize*, Lan Sluder, an American journalist who once was a business newspaper editor in New Orleans in the southern American state of

Louisiana, describes life in Belize in the following terms:

"To start with, Belize is simply beautiful. It is a place of incredible natural beauty, mint green or turquoise seas and emerald green forests, and the longest barrier reef in the Western and Northern Hemispheres, with more kinds of birds, butterflies, flowers, and trees than in all of the United States and Canada combined.

Massive ceiba trees and exotic cohune palms stand guard in rain forests where jaguars still roam free and toucans and parrots fly overhead.

Rivers, bays, and lagoons are rich with hundreds of different kinds of fish.

Belize is one of the world's wild frontiers, a kind of pint-sized, subtropical Alaska.

Belize also has an interesting mix of cultures, ethnicities, and heritages.

It's a dilemma, an enigma, and an exception to most of the rules of its region: an English-speaking country in a Spanish-speaking world, a British colony in Latin America, and a Caribbean culture in a Latino society.

With a stable, democratic government, Belizeans treasure their freedom, but politics is intensely personal and often cutthroat.

Belize is usually safe and friendly, but it can be dangerous; there are sharks on land, as well as in the sea. Theft is endemic.

Belize is a little country with big problems to overcome.

It has both corrupt politicians and proud bureaucrats who expect respect, not bribes.

It's a poor, developing country, but even so, it seems to pay more attention to the environment than do its richer neighbors to the north.

Belize is a nation in the making, but also a land with a 4,000-year history of achievement.

While Europe huddled in ignorance during the Dark

Ages, Belize was the center of an empire of wealth and sophistication and a land of a million people, four times the population of the country today.

The Maya were mathematicians, architects, and theologians of great skill, who erected buildings that still remain the tallest in the region.

Belize is probably not like any other place you've ever been.

Despite the palm trees, frost-free climate, and slow pace of daily life, it's not a land where the living is always easy. It's cheap or expensive, depending on how you choose to live.

You can't just move to Belize and vegetate in comfortable retirement or hide behind the gated walls of a housing development for expatriates.

It's not a place in which to make easy money, and it's all too easy here to lose the money you have.

Take a little bit of Africa, a little of Europe, a little of the Caribbean, a little of Mexico and Guatemala, and a little of the United States, and you almost have Belize.

Yet Belize is more than that.

You've probably heard someone say about a certain part of the world, 'I like it, but it is not for everyone.' Of course not.

Not everyone likes New York City, not everyone likes London or Montana or New Zealand or any other dot on the map. No place is for everyone. But Belize is really not for everyone.

Some years ago, I was a business newspaper editor in New Orleans. A real estate agent I interviewed one time told me he could tell within minutes of meeting a prospective new resident at the airport whether that person would like New Orleans.

He said that people either got off the plane complaining about the heat and humidity, swatting bugs, and yelling at workers to hurry up with their bags, in which case they immediately hated New Orleans; or else they were enchanted by this most storied and eccentric of American cities and fell in love with it from the moment they stepped off the plane.

Coming to Belize for the first time is a little like that. You arrive at a little airport at the edge of nowhere. The hot, humid air hits you like a steaming blanket. Inside the airport is a confusing mélange of people of every color and station in life, speaking many different languages, and everywhere you look is a mix of anxious tourists and laid-back locals.

En route to wherever you're going, you soon pass a wide, dark river that looks like something out of a Joseph Conrad novel.

You see run-down, pastel-colored shacks like those in Jamaica, unfinished concrete houses such as those in Mexico, and new homes with chain-link fences and signs in Chinese.

You pass by bars and brothels that would have attracted the famous novelist and jammed streets with rickety wood-frame buildings.

Just when you think you're ready to turn around and go back to where you came from, you catch a glimpse of an unbelievably blue sea, a group of friendly schoolchildren in khaki uniforms who wave and shout, or, perhaps, the mysterious Maya Mountains in the far distance.

Belize may not be for you. But then, maybe you are that one person in 10 who will fall in love with Belize, with all its failings and frustrations.

You won't find it paradise. You won't find it perfect. But you'll wish you'd found it sooner." - (Lan Sluder, excerpt from *Living Abroad in Belize*, Avalon Publishing Group, Inc., 2005, published as "Living Abroad in Belize," www.livingabroadin.com/Belize/belize.html).

Belize is not for everybody; nor is any other country in the world including the United States which many people consider to be "paradise on Earth."

Life can be hell anywhere on Earth.

Conclusion

PEOPLE who go to Belize, including tourists and other travellers, find it easy to fit in because of the country's great ethnic and racial diversity reflecting many lifestyles and cultures. There is a place for everybody in Belize. Its people came from everywhere round the globe.

There are people of European origin. There are people of African and Asian ancestry. And there are, of course, the indigenous people. There are also many people of mixed racial heritages. They all make Belize a rainbow nation of dazzling diversity.

The cultural and ethnic diversity is reflected in the different customs and traditions, languages, religions, foods, music and even how the people dress.

But this kind of diversity is also a source of strength, giving Belize its unique identity, and uniting its people as members of a rainbow nation.

Although different groups speak their own languages, they are also united by a common language, a form of pidgin English called Kriol.

Standard English is taught in all primary schools. But it's not used as much as Kriol is. It's use mainly for official purposes mainly in written form. It's written more than it's spoken; another distinctive feature of Belize.

Although there many distinct ethnic communities, the people mingle easily in many areas of life.

There is prejudice in Belize just as in all societies, many of which have been torn apart because of that. But that is not the case in Belize. The country does not have a history of violence ignited and fuelled by racial and ethnic hatred.

Yet there are lines drawn in intergroup relations and sometimes even in individual relationships, for example, involving intermarriage. Some people don't accept that although inter-racial marriage is common.

There are some areas – rural and urban – where members of different ethnic and racial groups coexist. But they always don't mingle for historical and cultural reasons. Prejudice is another reason.

However, the evolution of the country from colonial status to independence has had an ethnic component in terms of leadership. And it has played a key role in shaping Belize's national identity.

The party that led the country to independence was mainly Creole in terms of leadership. Even the first prime minister after the country won independence was Creole.

The leaders were urban-based and well-educated. But they were also mainly light-skinned, a distinctive factor which has had an impact on inter-ethnic relations in a country already divided along ethnic lines in terms of demographic composition and opportunities in life.

Yet there is no question that the country has made significant strides in terms of ethnic relations especially since independence. Post-colonial leaders wanted to build an integrated society that was all-inclusive in terms of rights regardless of one's identity. That was not the case in the past.

During colonial rule, the country was socially stratified to reflect ethnic and racial identities, with dark-skinned people of African origin being one of the most disadvantaged groups. Skin pigmentation was one of the prime determinants in the construction of this social and racial hierarchy.

Those differences have now been transformed into attributes of a society that attempts to harness the potential of all its people to build a truly rainbow nation

Still, it would be overly optimistic to say those differences no longer play a role in life. They do.

Traditionally, people in the rural areas are stratified along ethnic lines even if they already live in their own areas or ethnic enclaves. In urban areas, skin colour rather than ethnicity is the determining factor.

At the highest levels of the social and racial hierarchy are light-skinned Creoles known as "royal Creoles," Mestizos, East Indians, whites including immigrants from the United States, and Arabs from the Middle East. At the lowest levels are dark-skinned Kriols and Garifuna.

These divisions almost neatly coincide with one's station in life. Light-skinned people rule, have better jobs and other opportunities in life than dark-skinned ones, although many Belizeans with a dark complexion have also risen to the top through the decades.

But in general, dark-skinned Belizeans are poorer and less educated than light-skinned ones. And there are more light-skinned people among the Creole than there are among the Garifuna, the other major group of black Belizeans besides the Creole.

Although the Garifuna have distinguished themselves in the area of education, as an ethnic group they're still some of the poorest people in Belize, a condition which has forced many of them to immigrate to the United States and to other countries in search of better life.

And they provide one of the best examples of a people caught in the kind of predicament other people are trapped in: the desire to survive and thrive in their own country as individuals and as an ethnic and cultural group, while at the same time many of them have another desire, the desire to leave Belize in search of greener pastures.

191

The Garifuna acknowledge the imperative need to work together with other groups for their collective wellbeing within the country itself even if many of them have left and continue to leave Belize. But they are also determined to assert their identity as a separate ethnic and cultural entity in a multicultural society where every ethnic group is proud of it own identity and heritage and wants to be recognised as a unique part of the nation but also at the same time as an integral part of it.

The problems they face are also addressed by the group in their own ethno-cultural context in a way they may not be by other groups because of the differences in culture, historical experiences and contemporary necessities of the different ethnic groups in Belize.

The Garifuna National Council (NGC) articulates its position on a number of issues in the following terms:

"The Garifuna language is spoken in Garifuna communities scattered along the Caribbean coast of Nicaragua, Honduras, Guatemala and Belize. In all of these communities the forces of the current world order threaten to overwhelm the Garifuna language and culture if mitigating actions are not taken.

On April 12th, 1997 the 200th anniversary of the arrival of the Garifuna People in Central America was celebrated. Events surrounding the observances brought a new awareness to many of the circumstances surrounding our exile from St. Vincent, and the real reasons for the attempted genocide, as well as a new appreciation for the miracle of our survival.

While we managed to survive the inhuman treatment two hundred years ago and continue to exist today as a distinct group it is our view that our culture is now threatened.

The threat comes from ourselves as well as from some of the modern-day institutions that have a profound effect on us. The danger from within arises from the fact that we are fast losing the identity and cultural strength that enabled our ancestors to resist great hardships and deprivations. We learned and taught the history, language and culture of those who colonized us but are losing our own.

The erosion of the Garifuna language in Belize is particularly worrisome and the concern is expressed in all sectors of the Belizean Garifuna society – young and old. This threatens our value system and our existence as a people and there is a need to take action to stem the erosion as quickly as possible.

The erosion has affected our self-esteem and performance as a people. As a result, we are alienating our lands and are performing poorly in school.

The fact is that our language is still spoken and its use is widespread. However, it is only in one village – Hopkins – that young children still learn it as their native language.

There is an awareness of the fact that this very important part of our identity is beginning to slip away. This awareness is coupled with a feeling of helplessness as parents are blamed for not speaking it to their children even while they use the language among themselves.

In this climate, it is imperative that the National Garifuna Council (NGC) takes the lead in working out interventions aimed at arresting the loss of our language and other elements of our culture." – ((Institute for Social and Cultural Research (ISCR), National Institute of Culture & History, Belmopan City, Belize, "The Garifuna National Council: Its Achievements," 2010).

It goes on to state:

"NGC's mission is to advocate for and secure the rights, development, and culture of the Garifuna in Belize, while promoting economic sustainability, interracial harmony and maintaining traditional respect for the preservation of the environment....

The Garifuna people are struggling with issues of poverty and cultural survival. Maintenance of a vibrant language and oral tradition is essential to the identity of the Garifuna people....

Cultural preservation for the Garinagu is important for all generations, but no one is more important than working with young people to promote cultural pride, learning traditional customs, and have an opportunity to practice the Garifuna language.

Outside forces such as migration and adopting westernized philosophies and world view have eroded cultural values and traditions of the Garifuna in Belize. As Belize is a relatively small country, of only 300,000 persons, and only 15 per cent of the total population is Garifuna, cultural erosion is inevitable.

However, as Garinagu become part of the wider Belizean culture, it is important for them to embrace and learn their own special cultural traditions and how the Garifuna have contributed to the development of Belize.

As people move away from their traditional homes, they lose their traditional language. Garifuna is an oral language that makes it very susceptible to being lost and forgotten. Today, very few children speak Garifuna which is a precursor of the loss of language to come.

The rich history of the Garifuna culture is found in the language, the stories, and the songs. Once the language is lost, they will also lose their songs, stories, and history.

It is vital that the language be written so that it can be studied and written down. The revision and creation of a new dictionary will allow students to undertake the study of the language and hopefully, reverse the erosion that the language has seen in the past.

The contribution of the Garifuna culture and of the Garinagu to Belize is widely recognized to be disproportionate to their population size.

Garifuna teachers were renowned for their skills and

were relied upon by the Catholic Church in the propagation of modern education to all other ethnic groups in rural communities in the early 1900's.

Garinagu also constitute a major part of health workers, Police Department and the Defense Forces of Belize.

The music and dance is powerfully appealing and has today become synonymous with the Belizean identity.

But notwithstanding all these achievements, the Garinagu as a whole are largely recognized to be at the lower end of the economic spectrum and economic opportunities for the young are very minimal in the home communities in the southern part of Belize....

It is difficult to preserve cultural customs while fighting extreme poverty." – (Ibid.)

There is no question that the Garifuna are some of the poorest people in Belize. But it's the Maya who are the most disadvantaged. And the unemployment rate among them is the highest among all the ethnic groups in the country; so is the rate of poverty.

The Maya have another distinctive characteristic. Not only is the rate of poverty highest among them; their participation in the political and socioeconomic arenas is also the lowest among all the groups in Belize.

The Maya have one identity but they are also divided into two groups or subgroups: the Mopan and the Kekchi. There are some differences among them, including cultural, but they are basically the same people.

And although Belize is one country, it's not one in all fundamental respects. One of those areas is culture. Cultural diversity coincides with ethnicity.

Because of its cultural diversity, Belize does not have a single national culture, although the prevalence of Kriol – Belizean Creole – as a common language does in a way define Belizeans as a distinct group of people with their own identity.

Still, Belize is not a melting pot. It's multi-ethnic and multi-cultural with distinct group identities.

There are also forms of music which are identified with Belize. But they are also a fusion of other forms of music from outside, such as reggae and soca as well as calypso, although with a distinctly Belizean flavour.

It does not mean that Belizeans are not creative or innovative. They are what they are, and do what they do, because they are product of many cultures; which explains why there is such cultural fusion in the Belizean context. For example, many Belizeans have strong cultural traditions which go all the way back to Africa.

There are also the Maya, the indigenous people, with equally strong cultural roots and traditions, as well as others.

The culture of many Belizeans, especially Kriols, is strongly identified with the culture or cultures of the island nations in the Caribbean the majority of whose people are of African origin.

So, while it's true that Belize is a Central American nation, a significant part of its population is distinctively Caribbean in terms of cultural orientation and racial affinity.

The people who constitute this segment of the Belizean population identify their destiny as being inextricably linked with the destiny of their brethren in Jamaica, Trinidad and Tobago, Grenada, Barbados and other island nations in the region who are bound by a common African heritage.

Yet there are differences even among the Creole themselves. There is no single Creole identity in terms of race because there is no such race. Probably the only thing which unites Creoles as a "race" is their common African identity.

There has been so much racial intermingling that it's impossible to use a biological category to identify Creoles except those who have clearly identifiable African features.

The same applies to the other major group, the Mestizo. Many of them are so white that they hardly have any Mayan blood. Yet they claim Mayan ancestry as much as "typical" Mayans or Mayan-looking Mestizos do.

Belize is a mosaic of races and cultures but probably of cultures more than races. That is why, for example, the Garifuna are culturally different from the Creole in spite of the fact that both share a common African heritage.

There are black Belizeans, – and "black" Belizeans, a dichotomy that is more important than race in the Belizean context. Even the common racial identity they share as a people of African origin has not been able to transcend that.

There are dark-skinned Creoles, light-skinned Creoles, dark-skinned Garifunas, and light-skinned Garifunas, all claiming to be black even if some of them are heavily mixed or don't look black at all. They are also divided by culture, of course, Creole versus Garifuna, and even by history.

Still, Belize is one of the best examples of stable multicultural – and multiracial – societies in the world. It's also one of the best examples of ethno-cultural harmony.

But it's also far from being an ideal society where people of different races, cultures and ethnicities have transcended their differences in spite of the relative peace and harmony that exists in this "paradise" in Central America.

198

CPSIA information can be obtained
at www.ICGtesting.com
Printed in the USA
LVOW01s1443170117
521252LV00008B/951/P

9 789987 160471